"TENNIS KING EQUATION2"
"BEYOND THE VORTEX"
BY MARK JOHNS

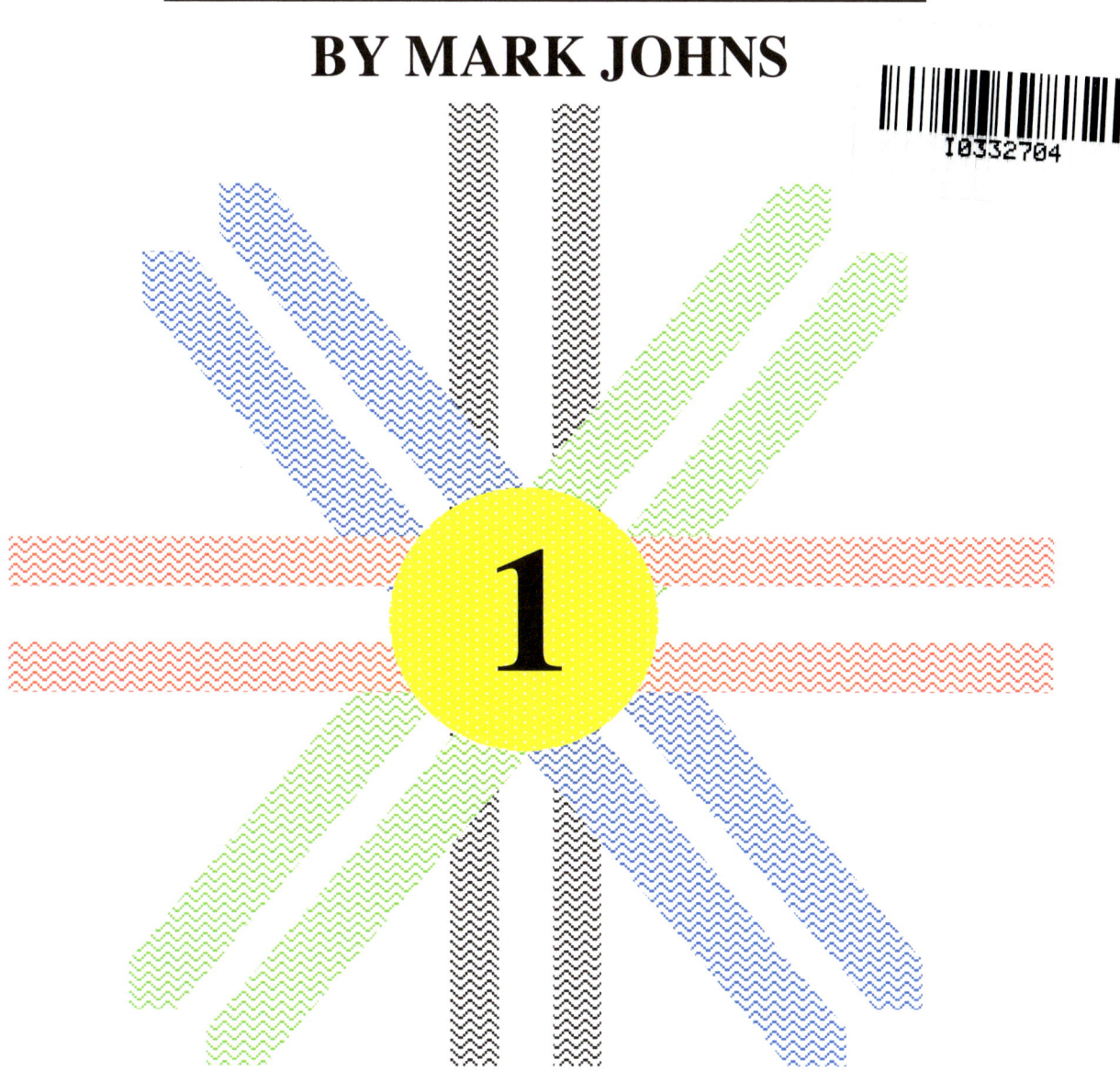

**BEYOND THE VORTEX
WE DON'T TRY TO HIT THE BALL BECAUSE**

"THERE IS NO BALL!"

TENNIS KING EQUATION ^{2} "BEYOND THE VORTEX"
WHEN YOU WANT TO UNDERSTAND THE WORLD OF TENNIS

the Tennis King Equation2

"BEYOND THE VORTEX"

copyright © 2008 by Mark Johns

All rights reserved. No part of this publication may be reproduced or transmitted in any form or by any means, electronic or mechanical, including photocopy, recording or any information storage and retrieval system, without the permission in writing from the author. Any request for permission should be e-mailed to: mark@TheTennisKing.com

TENNIS KING EQUATION^2 "BEYOND THE VORTEX"
WHEN YOU WANT TO UNDERSTAND THE WORLD OF TENNIS

"TENNIS KING EQUATION 2" WRITTEN BY HEAD PRO MARK JOHNS ESPECIALLY FOR YOU.

THE TENNIS KING EQUATION2

THE EVOLUTION OF A PLAYER'S GAME NEVER HAS TO STOP.

#		#	
1	CHAPTER 1: TENNIS KING EQUATION2	69	PAY THE TOLL & GET ON THE BRIDG
3	TABLE OF CONTENTS	71	WHAT IS THE PREBRIDGE INDUCTION ?
5	WHEN YOU WANT TO UNDERSTAND	73	SCALAR SCOPE THE VORTE
7	CHAPTER 2: 1ST DIMENSION OF TIME	75	USE A SCALAR BAR TO CREATE THE SHOT
9	WELCOME TO THE 1ST DIMENSION OF TIME	77	MICRO AND MACRO MANAGEMENT
11	INTRODUCING THE "BLACK HOLE" THEORY	79	MICRO AND MACRO BAR CODES
13	HOW TO CAPTURE COMPRESSION	81	THE VECTORIZATION OF THE VORTE
15	WHAT IS A "BLACK HOLE" REALLY?	83	THE "GOLDEN TRIANGLE" THEORY
17	THE VORTEX GIVES YOU THE VECTC	85	"RING FOR SERVICE" TO HOLD YOUR SERVE
19	YOU MUST HOLD THE VECTOR OPEN	87	VIRTUAL VECTOR "C" VISION
21	PICK UP THE POST IMPACT SIGNAL	89	ASTRAL PROJECTION IS AS SIMPLE AS "A-B-C"
23	CAPTURE THE CURVE	91	TO "B" OR NOT TO "B" - THAT IS THE QUESTIO
25	W.W.W. = YOUR GAME ONLINE	93	WANT TO GET THERE FAST - TAKE THE "B" LI
27	PLAYING IS AS EASY AS TAKING A SNAPSHOT	95	THE DOUBLE "D" WORKS FINE FOR N
29	A PHOTON PHOTO WORKS THE BEST	97	NO TWO BALL PRINTS ARE ALIKE
31	"THERE CAN BE ONLY ONE	99	THE "GREAT TRIANGLE" FOR A SURE SHOT
33	"MAKING TIME STAND STILL"	101	THE ANGULAR COMPRESSION & DILATION OF TIME
35	CHAPTER 3: TIME AND SPACE	103	TAKE THE TUNNEL - IT'S FASTER THAN THE BRIDGE
37	"TIME OVER SPACE" PARADIGM	105	TUNNEL VISION & TIME TUNNELING
39	FIND THE BLACK HOLE	107	"LOAD-LOCK-HOLD" IS ALL YOU HAVE TO DO
41	CONSCIOUS COMPOSITION	109	STREAMLINING THE TUNNEL'S TRIANGLE
43	THE MULTI VERSE IS HERE	111	CHAPTER 5: THE EYE OF TIME
45	PERCEPTION OF TIME EQUALS SOM	113	THE "VORTICAL FLOW" AND "THE EYE OF TIN
47	SYNCHRONIZATION OF THE WAVES	115	GET INTO "THE EYE OF TIME"
49	THE SPECTRUM OF FOCUS INSTENSITY	117	ZOOM INTO THE "VORTICAL FLOW" SPECTRU
51	DON'T TOUCH THE SNAKE !	119	DEVELOP THE URGE TO CHANNEL THE SURGE
53	QUANTUM SCALAR DYNAMICS	121	YOU HAVE TO GO "NUCLEAR" TO BE ATOMIC
55	THE VORTEX AXIS IS THE "BRIDGE"	123	TO CREATE AN IMPACT - STEP INTO THE RING
57	TAKE THE ALPHA-BETA TIME TUNNI	125	THE SHOT'S NUCLEUS = THE NUCLEAR CLOCI
59	CROSSOVERS AND ANOREADERS	127	CHAPTER 6: VORTIVISION AND VECTOR FIELDS
61	ON THE "WALL OF TIME"	129	VORTIVISION TRACKS VORTICAL FLOW
63	CHAPTER 4: FOCUS MODELS	131	VORTIVISION - NUCLEAR RING - THE FUTURE
65	OPERATING SYSTEMS & FOCUS MODELS	133	THE VECTOR FIELD TRIGGERS THE ALPHA-BE
67	STEP INTO THE VORTEX	135	THE TENNIS KING EQUATION2 - CONCLUSION

TENNIS KING EQUATION^2 "BEYOND THE VORTEX"

WHEN YOU WANT TO UNDERSTAND THE WORLD OF TENNIS

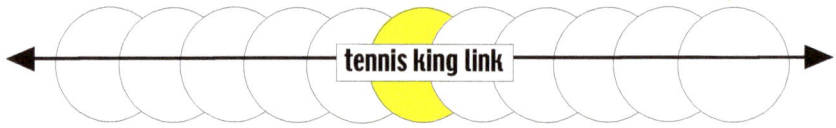

HOW YOU CAN LINK UP

"READ & REPLY"
questions or thoughts welcome
mark@TheTennisKing.com

In the "read & reply" box is my e-mail address. Please feel free to contact me at any time. If you have a question or thought e-mail it and I will respond.

These book projects initially started out as individual note pages pertaining to my on court lessons so my students could fortify their understanding.

The more notes I created the better I played. The students also got into it. They enjoyed the information and it generated improvement in their games. The fact that both my students and I were playing better was very exciting.

I continued to record my observations during my tournament matches on the change overs and discovered a wealth of knowledge. The writing of notes on the "change over" created a certain objectivity which allowed me to see a lot more then I would have if I just toweled off and plunged on.

After thirteen years of note taking I had amassed enough information to to create these tennis books. The evolution of the "Tennis King Equation" series has taken on a life of it's own. At times this quantum perspective of tennis seems so strange, but it is very interesting and stimulating.

If you are inspired by any of the subjects in the "Tennis King Equation2" let's talk. We can extend the tennis horizon by communicating.

TENNIS KING EQUATION^2 "BEYOND THE VORTEX"
WHEN YOU WANT TO UNDERSTAND THE WORLD OF TENNIS

"TENNIS KING EQUATION 2" WRITTEN BY HEAD PRO MARK JOHNS ESPECIALLY FOR YOU.

WHEN YOU WANT TO UNDERSTAND

FORGET ABOUT WHAT YOU ALREADY KNOW AND SEEK THE UNKNOWN

"When you want to understand the world, you need to look beyond normal and narrow limits of the human experience. When you go past the limits of up and down, time and space, you will find a uniformity where extraordinary things are happening. Things that in ordinary everyday life you don't know exist. For me this is the fascination of science." - Francis Crick, co-discover of "DNA"

This quote by the Nobel prize winning scientist sums it up very nicely. If you want to improve your tennis game you need to expand the limits of what you see. The purpose of this book "Tennis King Equation2" is to capitalize on the information in the first "Tennis King Equation" (TKE) and further extend your appreciation of our metaphysical tennis experience.

In the first book (TKE) I focused on explaining the "ball orientation" and the "self orientation". The intention of showing the player the differences between the "event" level and the "composition" level results in the development of very specific visual references and focus techniques. It may be helpful before a player attempts to tackle the more abstract concepts found in this book to read the first Tennis King Equation to create a strong foundation of understanding for this usual approach to the game of tennis.

In the Tennis King Equation2 the object is to acquaint the player with the idea of the "force fields" that move the tennis ball. The identification of these fields and the ability to read them will make the "ball orientation" outdated (now there is no ball). The fields of energy at work in the tennis world are experienced over and over again. This allows the player the opportunity to learn the patterns of energy flow and develop responses that precedes the presence of the physical ball.

The physical realm is the residue of the dimension of time and there are many dimensions of time. An example of this is found today in quantum physics which offers the currently popular "string theory" with it's eleven dimensions of time. This multidimensional time concept means that we are capable learning to play tennis in time rather than physical space and be much more effective. Our game will improve with the mastery of each new level of time. With each new level comes a new and deeper understanding of physical reality.

The concept of multidimensional time allows for unlimited expansion in our tennis.
⬅———————— *tennis king "physics"* ————————➡
This understanding explains why top players make it look so easy.

TENNIS KING EQUATION ^{2} "BEYOND THE VORTEX"
WHEN YOU WANT TO UNDERSTAND THE WORLD OF TENNIS

Tennis players are very aware of the different levels of play. The idea that these different levels of expertise represent the "dimension of time" that a player responses from is fascinating. This means by simply recognizing the next time frame we increase our performance level.

The recognition of a new level of time is achieved by learning the critical focus landmarks in that dimension. Once you program your responses to these new references your game changes and performance improves.

I find it very interesting to think of players residing in different dimensions of time and this alone determines their level of play.

In which level of time does Roger Fedrer reside?

TENNIS KING EQUATION ^{2} "BEYOND THE VORTEX"
WHEN YOU WANT TO UNDERSTAND THE WORLD OF TENNIS

"TENNIS KING EQUATION 2" WRITTEN BY HEAD PRO MARK JOHNS ESPECIALLY FOR YOU.

2

"THE 1ST DIMENSION"

TENNIS KING EQUATION^2 "BEYOND THE VORTEX"
OPTIMAL PLAY THROUGH "ENERGY FIELD" RECOGNITION

The Tennis King terminology:

compression event = when the ball bounces or is hit. It compresses and decompresses for .005 -.008 seconds.

vortex = space between the ball and racket just before they impact.

vector = an address on the ball or in time that sends the shot to a specific destination.

focus sight-line = a specific line of sight that highlights certain visual references.

photon address = a vector address that lights up in your mind to help you determine the correct address.

"TENNIS KING EQUATION 2" WRITTEN BY HEAD PRO MARK JOHNS ESPECIALLY FOR YOU.

WELCOME TO THE 1ST DIMENSION OF TIME

THE BOUNCE BEFORE YOU IMPACT THE BALL IS THE FRONTIER OF TIME

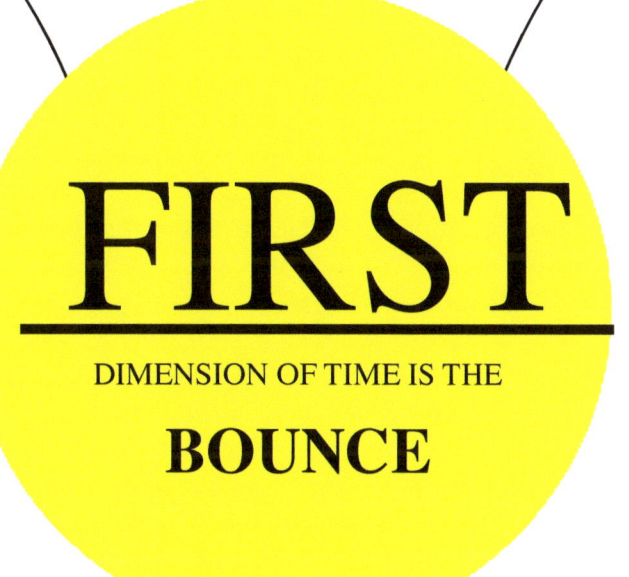

FIRST
DIMENSION OF TIME IS THE
BOUNCE

You may have seen a million bounces during your tennis career.

←——— *tennis king "physics"* ———→

Now when you see the bounce - you will be looking into the future.

TENNIS KING EQUATION ² "BEYOND THE VORTEX"
OPTIMAL PLAY THROUGH "ENERGY FIELD" RECOGNITION

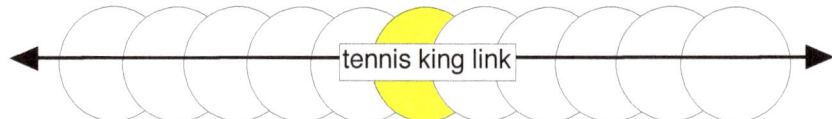

A typical player scenario consists of an internal dialogue where the player reminds himself to watch the ball.

Maybe it is a little more evolved than "watch the ball". It could be watch the ball into the racket. When an mistake occurs the player attaches a "cause for error" to the missed shot and that is I did not watch the ball.

Forget about the ball - there is no ball!

TENNIS KING EQUATION ^{2} "BEYOND THE VORTEX"
OPTIMAL PLAY THROUGH "ENERGY FIELD" RECOGNITION

Now when you see the bounce - you will be looking into the future.

"TENNIS KING EQUATION 2" WRITTEN BY HEAD PRO MARK JOHNS ESPECIALLY FOR YOU.

INTRODUCING THE "BLACK HOLE" THEORY

YOU CAN NOW FORGET ABOUT WATCHING THE BALL

The diagram above is a "compression point" The compression point is the location of the ball changing direction as a result of an impact with a racquet or the ground.

The compression point above is a bounce of the ball on the court. The yellow rings represent the ball compressing and the black dot indicates the force of gravity on the ball.

This "black hole" of gravity was created the moment the ball was struck by the opponent's racket. The black hole resides on the court's surface, it is the bounce's location. It will remain unchanging and stationary throughout the flight of the ball. The compression point is easier to see than the moving ball because it is stationary.

When a player observes the opponent's vortex (the diminishing space between the ball and the racquet) before the ball is hit, the location of where the ball is going to bounce becomes available. This is the "black hole" or future compression point of the ball being struck.

Observing a "moving" object is more difficult then observing a "still" object.
⬅ ——— ***tennis king "physics"*** ———➡
Hitting a "still" object is easier then hitting a "moving" object.

TENNIS KING EQUATION² "BEYOND THE VORTEX"
OPTIMAL PLAY THROUGH "ENERGY FIELD" RECOGNITION

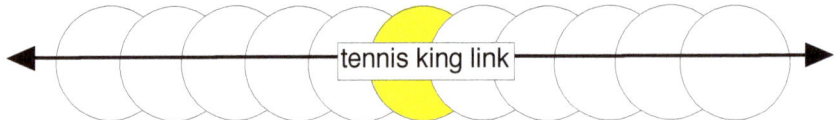

The idea that the tennis player need not watch the ball is unheard of. When confronted with this statement the experienced player thinks that you are joking or crazy.

In The Tennis King Equation2 - "Beyond the Vortex" I am going to demonstrate that watching the ball is less effective than observing the flow of energy that the ball represents.

The energy field that controls the actions of the ball is ever present and understandable. A player who can read the "field" realizes a future action in the current moment. The field is constant and the ball is momentary.

Responding to the field is easier the responding to the ball.

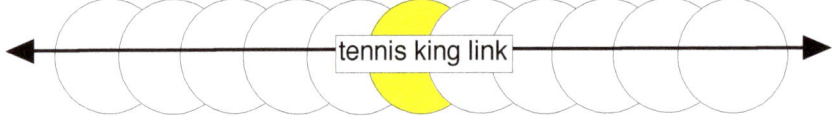

"TENNIS KING EQUATION 2" WRITTEN BY HEAD PRO MARK JOHNS ESPECIALLY FOR YOU.

HOW TO CAPTURE COMPRESSION

CAPTURING COMPRESSION IS LESS STRESSFUL THEN HITTING A BALL

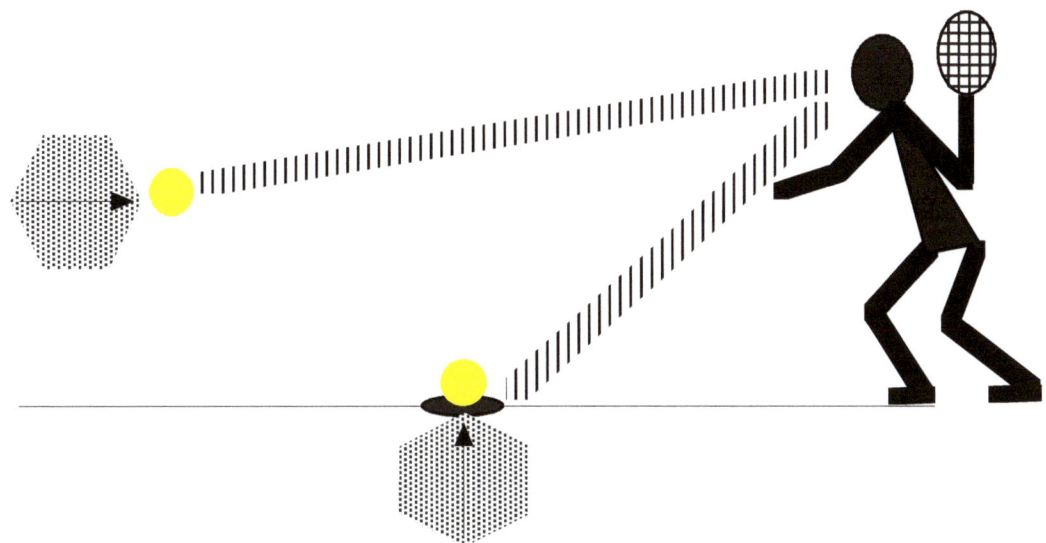

The concept of "capturing" compression is a visual focus technique of viewing the opponent's vortex and then viewing a mentally constructed pre-bounce compression point of where the ball will bounce. The player's direct focus is never on the ball.

The vortex and the compression point are stationary force fields existing in the dimension of time preceding the actual compression events of the opponent's impact and the bounce.

The idea of not watching the ball relates to the placement of your direct focus. The player maintaining a constant effort to follow the ball is prone toward a neurotic obsession to not lose sight of the ball. This creates stress based on the fear of not being able to kept up the vigil. To see the vortex and compression point is not as demanding and so it is not as stressful.

The appearance of physical reality is the result of the preceding force field.

⬅ ——— ***tennis king "physics"*** ———➡

If we play the force field we will be ahead of the ball.

TENNIS KING EQUATION^2 "BEYOND THE VORTEX"

OPTIMAL PLAY THROUGH "ENERGY FIELD" RECOGNITION

The ball is the force field's indicator. It is merely a marker for a flow of energy that exists during a rally between two players.

The player responding to the ball will have missed the flow of energy because when you swing at the ball - it is not going to be where your swing is directed. It will have moved forward in time - causing the player to suffer a miss timed swing.

As the rally increases in velocity the discrepancy in timing between the ball and the racket increases to the result of the eventual unforced error

TENNIS KING EQUATION ^{2} "BEYOND THE VORTEX"
OPTIMAL PLAY THROUGH "ENERGY FIELD" RECOGNITION

"TENNIS KING EQUATION 2" WRITTEN BY HEAD PRO MARK JOHNS ESPECIALLY FOR YOU.

WHAT IS A "BLACK HOLE" REALLY?

WITH BLACK HOLE TECHNOLOGY WE REALIZE THAT REALITY IS IN THE MIND.

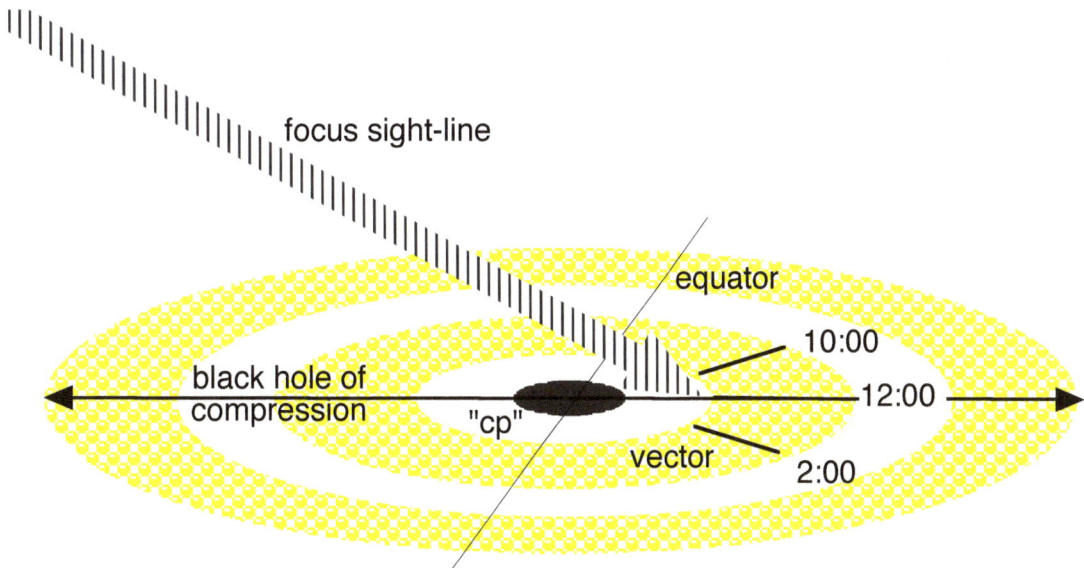

The pre-bounce diagram above has all the familiar "ball orientation" characteristics found in "The Tennis King Equation 1" which by the way I feel is a "must read" to enable you to comprehend "black hole technology". The only difference is they now reside in the black hole's "force field" of the pre-bounce. We see the shadow of compression, the equator, the vector and the vector's addresses and finally we see our own focus sight-line.

A very bright young student (11 years old) asked me if the black hole is really there? Is it on the court and do you really see it? I explained to him that all of this is a mental construction in our imagination that is transposed on to the court's surface. I also told him that it is "very real" and if you see it you will play much better than if you don't see it. He was satisfied with this answer.

The concept of the black hole is a figment of your imagination - but it does work.

⬅ ——— **tennis king "physics"** ——— ➡

You see the black hole as a pre-bounce compression point on the court.

TENNIS KING EQUATION ² "BEYOND THE VORTEX"
OPTIMAL PLAY THROUGH "ENERGY FIELD" RECOGNITION

The force fields found in the vortex and the vector are pre-physical events that reside in the time preceding the opponent's impact and the bounce of the ball, but they are realized in our mind's imagination.

Our ability to use "mental construction" to generate physical response is the way our mind does everything involving a physical response.

In "The Tennis King Equation2" we are able to arrest the conscious mind's tendency to interfere with the subconscious's physical response by developing specific references in time.

"TENNIS KING EQUATION 2" WRITTEN BY HEAD PRO MARK JOHNS ESPECIALLY FOR YOU.

THE VORTEX GIVES YOU THE VECTOR

THE VORTEX TO VECTOR RELATIONSHIP IS THE ULTIMATE TENNIS EQUATION

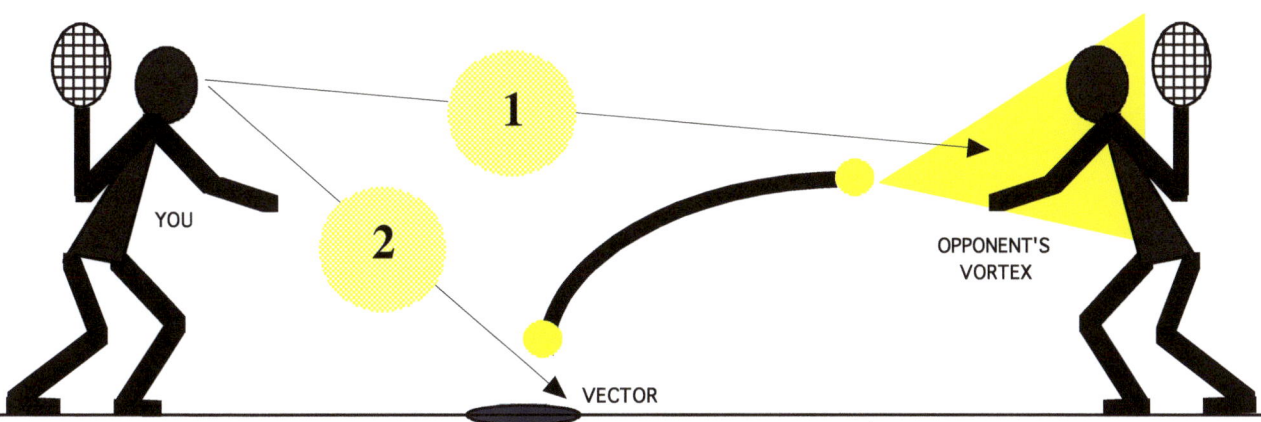

The vortex and the vector are two visual references which reveal two impending compression events (the opponent's impact & the bounce) which are actually force field at work.

The simplification of the "Tennis King Equation" is the recognition of this most essential "vortex to vector" formula. The player's response to these pre-compression events is to generate sight-lines into these force fields.

The vortex sight-line (#1) is the source of the information that reveals the compression point on the court where the opponent's shot will bounce. Once you have vortexed the opponent's shot the next assignment is to produce the vector sight-line (#2) deep into the black hole of compression. This sight-line can be manipulated to the black hole's front circumference where the vector resides. This vector has all of the addresses for shots you want to hit.

The vector address shows itself as a photon lighting up and it guides the subconscious to swing to it without hesitation. This division of labor between the conscious mind that produces the sight-lines and subconscious mind which generates the swing insures a flawless and stress free physical response.

Establishing the vortex and vector sight lines are done in your conscious mind.

← tennis king "physics" →

Hitting the ball is your subconscious mind's responsibility.

TENNIS KING EQUATION ^{2} "BEYOND THE VORTEX"

OPTIMAL PLAY THROUGH "ENERGY FIELD" RECOGNITION

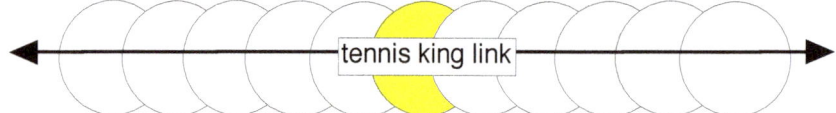

The focus sight-line is the player's response to the reoccurring circumstance of needing to hit the ball during a rally.

The quality of the sight-line is measured by the precision of it's placement into the opponent's vortex and the quickness of how fast it can get there.

The intensity of the sight-line determines how much physical energy that will be released into the swing. A soft focus produces a soft shot and a hard focus will hit a harder shot.

The ultimate measure of a player is the focus sight-line he produces.

"TENNIS KING EQUATION 2" WRITTEN BY HEAD PRO MARK JOHNS ESPECIALLY FOR YOU.

YOU MUST HOLD THE VECTOR OPEN

VISUALLY HOLDING ON TO THE VECTOR ADDRESS TILL THE SWING COMES THROUGH

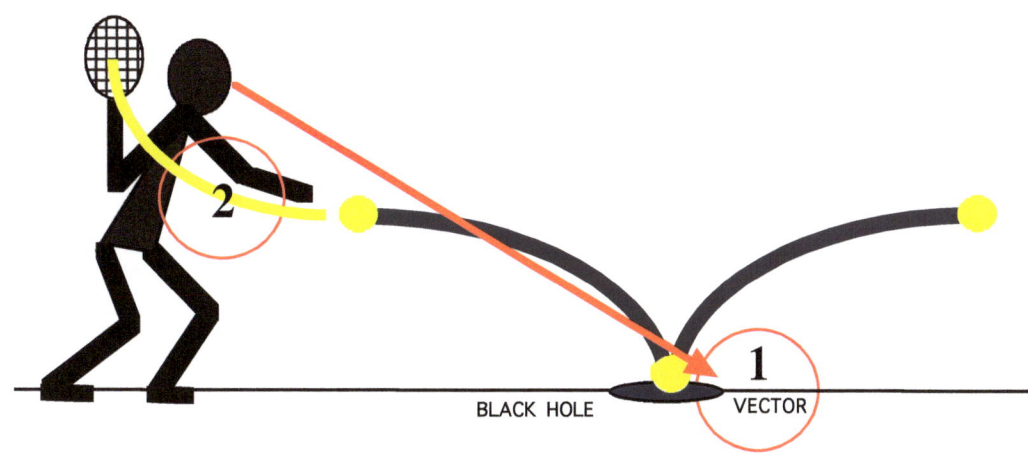

The black hole vector (bhv) is located in the front circumference of the black hole. The black hole is the force field of gravity pulling the ball down into the bounce. It is realized by players who have the ability to read force fields. The opponent's vortex (another force field) provides the coordinates of the black hole and the black hole's vector.

In the diagram #1 illustrates the "bhv" and the #2 represents the physical swing directed at the vector. The concept of swinging directly into the vector of the black hole is counter intuitive. The "ball" represents the usual visual reference that most players pursue in creating the shot. In black hole technology the ball represents "old news". The ball is merely the history of a force field expended and to play the ball means you must employ your energy to hit the shot.

The player uses the vortex information to create the location of the "bhv" and once the vector is seen the player swings directly into it. This allows the the ball's energy to motivate the shot. It is critical for the player to "*hold the image of the vector open in the conscious mind*" till the ball comes off the player's rackct during the follow through of the shot. This results in the successful swing based on the information found in the vector and prevents the conscious mind from trying to hit the moving "ball" rather then the stationary black hole vector.

Sight-line production is going to obtain the information needed to hit the ball.

⬅ *tennis king "physics"* ➡

Holding the vector open with the sight-line will allow the swing to hit through the ball.

TENNIS KING EQUATION ^{2} "BEYOND THE VORTEX"
OPTIMAL PLAY THROUGH "ENERGY FIELD" RECOGNITION

The vector address in the black-hole is a conscious minded effort to realize where the ball will bounce and how you should approach hitting that ball. This is possible by the vortex information collected at your opponent's impact.

The concept of holding the vector open to allow the swing to come through the impact is a focus technique to arrest the conscious mind from trying to hit the ball. By occupying the consciousness with the job of seeing and holding the vector address till the shot is done we are able to allow the subconscious mind to do it's. The swing and hitting the ball is a subconscious function.

When you are busy holding the vector address open - you don't see the ball!

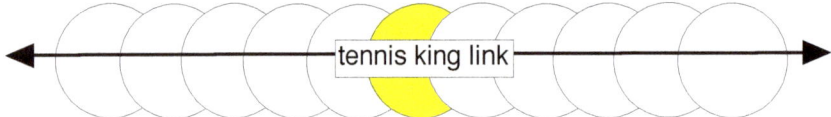

TENNIS KING EQUATION^2 "BEYOND THE VORTEX"
OPTIMAL PLAY THROUGH "ENERGY FIELD" RECOGNITION

"TENNIS KING EQUATION 2" WRITTEN BY HEAD PRO MARK JOHNS ESPECIALLY FOR YOU.

PICK UP THE POST IMPACT SIGNAL

HOLDING THE VECTOR ADDRESS TILL THE SWING PASSES THROUGH THE BALL ALLOWS YOU TO DO IT

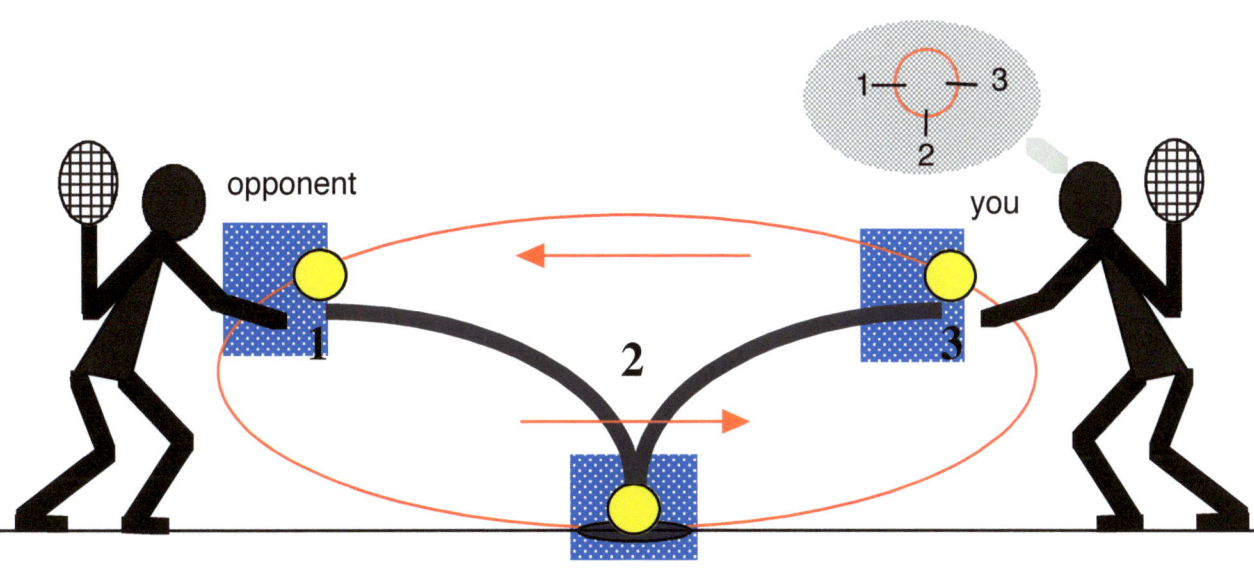

The post impact signal (p.i.s.) is the final awareness the you realize while impacting the ball. The mental effort of keeping the vector open allows the swing to come through the shot and the p.i.s. to be collected along with the very important information it represents.

The post impact signal (#3) is the bio-feed back experienced as the ball comes off the your racket detailing where the ball is going to go next. The location of the ball's next bounce revealed permits the you to recycle the ready position appropriate to where the next shot will be hit from. This ready position is defined as you move to the center point of the two possible angles that can be hit by the opponent from this specific bounce location.

The post impact signal also puts you right into the up coming vortex (#1) of the opponent's next shot. This is how you mentally work the 1-2-3 formation as a progressive state of mind that moves from one visual reference point to the next allowing you to detect the changing forces in the energy field which moves the ball. This is the "time over space" equation.

The post impact signal is only available if the player keeps his head in the impact,

⟵ ***tennis king "physics"*** ⟶

The post impact signal is felt as much as it is seen as the ball comes off the hit.

TENNIS KING EQUATION ^{2} "BEYOND THE VORTEX"

OPTIMAL PLAY THROUGH "ENERGY FIELD" RECOGNITION

The post impact signal is easily missed. The player can watch the ball into the racket or feel the contact of the ball and believe this event is over and then move the focus forward to see the results of the shot.

This is the reason the player needs to stay with the impact till the ball emerges from the racket. By doing so the player maintains a physical posture that stabilizes the impact and also allows for the collection of information found in the post impact signal.

When hitting the tennis ball - "haste makes waste"!

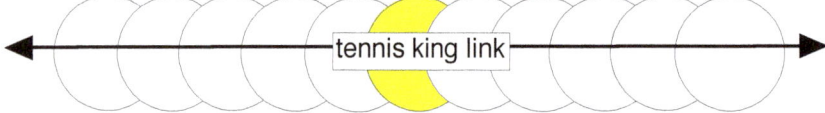

"TENNIS KING EQUATION 2" WRITTEN BY HEAD PRO MARK JOHNS ESPECIALLY FOR YOU.

CAPTURE THE CURVE

SEEING THE "CURVED" CIRCUMFERENCE OF THE BALL'S VECTOR IS YOUR OBJECTIVE

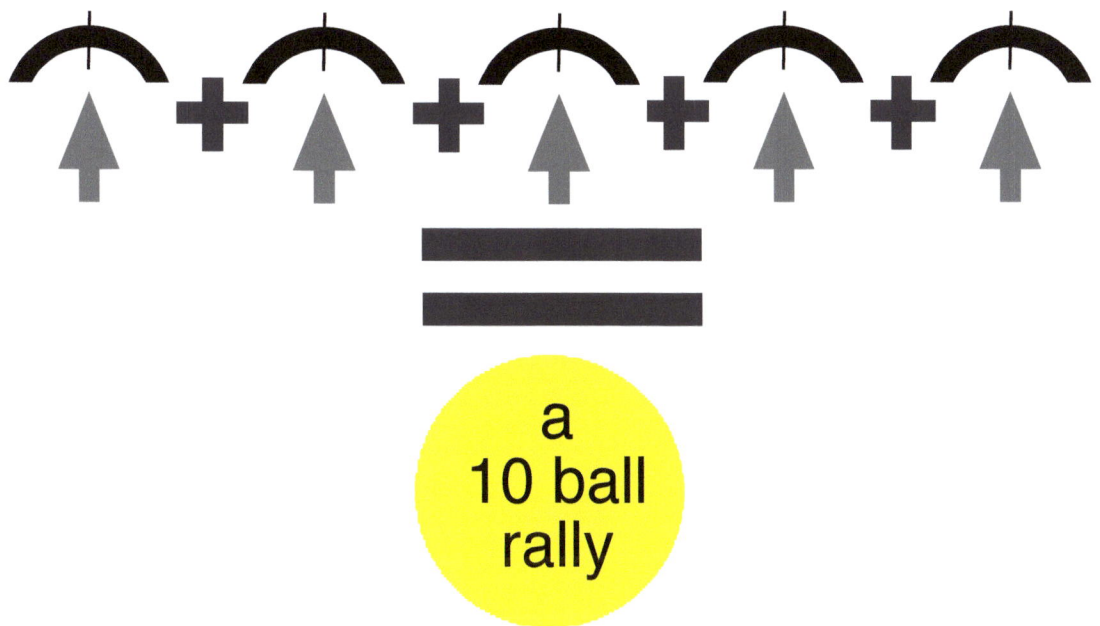

The simplicity of a concept can generate the level of it's function. The diagram above is defined by 5 vector addresses (the forward curve of the ball's circumference) in the compression of the ball at the bounce. A more elevated perspective is 5 vector addresses in the pre compression point of the blackhole and this equals (=) a 10 impact rally. The ability to be able to hit 5 shots without error seems to represent a defining moment in the development of the player.

The idea that a focus can see a series of 5 vector addresses is simple and easy. This will eliminate the stress of trying to make it happen. Once a player equates the vector address with the impact the need to try and hit the ball disappears.

The number of variables relates to the level of stress in a project.
← *tennis king* "*physics*" →
The reduction of variables is the way a player will reduce emotional stress.

TENNIS KING EQUATION² "BEYOND THE VORTEX"
OPTIMAL PLAY THROUGH "ENERGY FIELD" RECOGNITION

The player has but one true opponent. That opponent is the "mind" in a negative state. The ability or not to generate the correct perspective is equal to the player's potential. Accepting this idea will simplify everything that follows.

The attitude of the player with this "mind orientation" is less stressed than the player attempting to produce external physical results. Establish an order of priority with the "state of mind" being number "1" and the rest falls into line.

If you take care of the mind first - it will be able to take care of you.

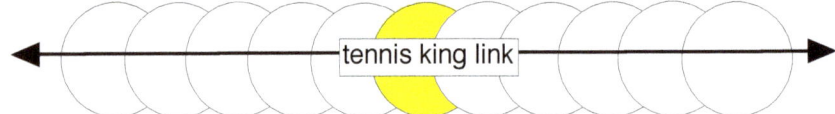

"TENNIS KING EQUATION 2" WRITTEN BY HEAD PRO MARK JOHNS ESPECIALLY FOR YOU.

W.W.W. = YOUR GAME ONLINE

THE 3 Ws = WHERE - WHAT - WHY WILL KEEP YOUR GAME ONLINE AND HUMMING

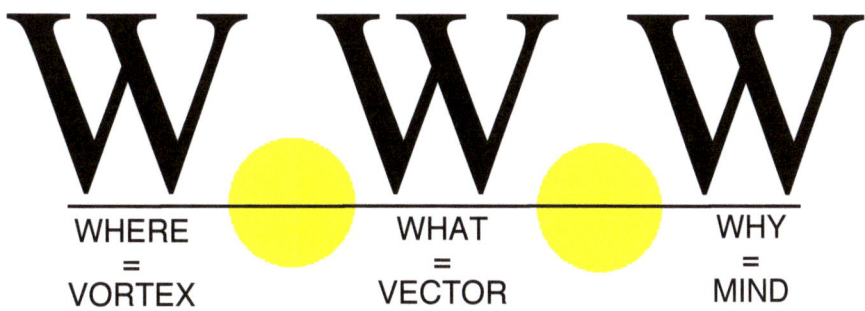

WHERE	WHAT	WHY
=	=	=
VORTEX	VECTOR	MIND

The only 3 words a player needs are "where"-"what"-"why". The 3 "w"s are the basic tools of the player's mind. A scalpel in the hands of the surgeon. Any situation that occurs can be resolved by using one of the 3 "w"s. This is how it works.

WHERE: by asking the vortex "where" we receive the location of the opponent's shot destination. This is how we move out of "space" into the first dimension of "time".

WHAT: by observing the "where" we are able to perceive the "what" as in the form of a vector address. The address in the vector is produced by asking "what".

WHY: the "why" comes into play whenever an error occurs. Immediately insert the "why" after the error to avert concentration breakdown and to reestablish the correct sequencing of mental references. This will keep your game online and humming.

All you need to play excellent tennis is the "where - what - why" questions.

⬅ *tennis king "physics"* ➡

By asking these questions you direct the pressure off of yourself and into the force field.

TENNIS KING EQUATION^2 "BEYOND THE VORTEX"
OPTIMAL PLAY THROUGH "ENERGY FIELD" RECOGNITION

The "www" concept is the ultimate "simple formula" for a successful state of mind. The "3w formula" covers all the bases without complicating everything.

It takes practice to edit the consciousness down to the "3w formula". The first step is to put it to work and watch it work. Once you believe it can work for you, the rest of tennis project starts to make sense.

If it is not relevant to the "3w formula" it's just not important!

TENNIS KING EQUATION² "BEYOND THE VORTEX"
OPTIMAL PLAY THROUGH "ENERGY FIELD" RECOGNITION

"TENNIS KING EQUATION 2" WRITTEN BY HEAD PRO MARK JOHNS ESPECIALLY FOR YOU.

PLAYING IS AS EASY AS TAKING A SNAPSHOT

A MINI SECOND SNAPSHOT OF THE VORTEX AND THE VECTOR IS ALL YOU HAVE TO SEE.

Many players over focus from one impact to the next. This effort not to lose sight of the ball is total overkill - it's like a beginner trumpet player blowing into the horn as hard as he can all the time. A more realistic and less exhausting perspective is generate two small snapshots of focus at the opponent's vortex and then at the vector on your bounce. This will save an enormous amount of mental energy and create a more effective physical response.

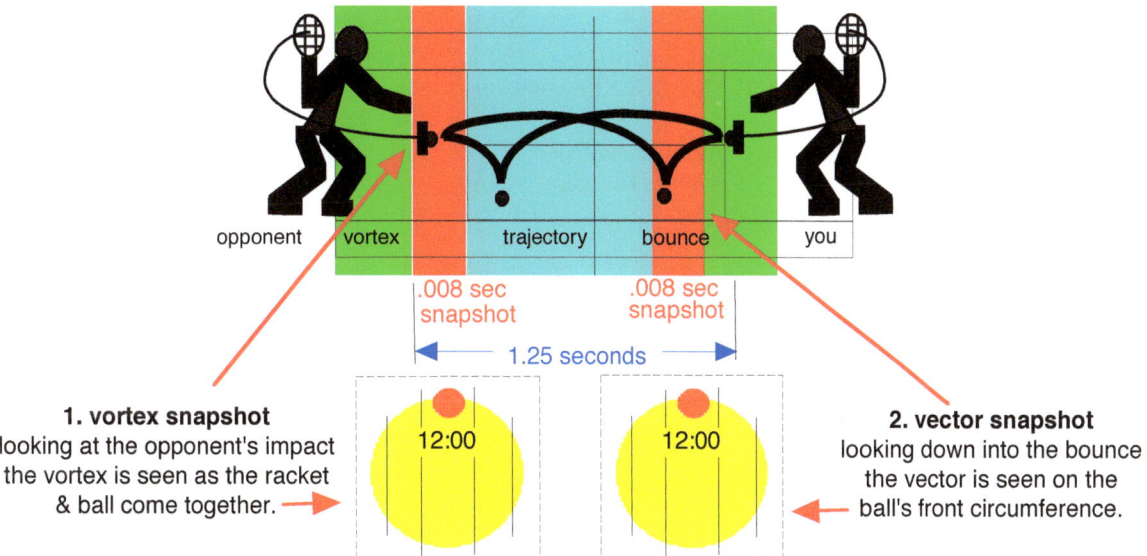

1. vortex snapshot
looking at the opponent's impact the vortex is seen as the racket & ball come together.

2. vector snapshot
looking down into the bounce the vector is seen on the ball's front circumference.

The vortex snapshot of the opponent's impact will reveal the bounce's address and allow you to move your focus forward to the bounce. It is here things get interesting. The vector address is found on the front circumference of the bounce. This vector address is your next snapshot. You take the snapshot and hold it in your consciousness until the after the ball leaves your impact. The effect of holding the snapshot during the entire impact is that you will not see any of the actual impact at all.
The info from this .008 second vector snapshot is all that is needed to hit the shot.

Average impact to impact time is 1.25 seconds - compression is only .008 seconds.

⟵ *tennis king "physics"* ⟶

Focusing for .008 seconds twice is much easier then a full 1.25 seconds

TENNIS KING EQUATION² "BEYOND THE VORTEX"
OPTIMAL PLAY THROUGH "ENERGY FIELD" RECOGNITION

The snapshot is a mini second recognition of the ball in a compression event. The amount of energy required to produce this vision is small and not at all neurotic.

Players are extremely motivated to perform well and this causes a tendency to over focus. The player that knows how to focus and when to focus will defeat the player who over focuses. The concept of "less is more" applies very well in this instance.

The snapshot is the mental effort that creates the shot.

TENNIS KING EQUATION ^{2} "BEYOND THE VORTEX"
OPTIMAL PLAY THROUGH "ENERGY FIELD" RECOGNITION

"TENNIS KING EQUATION 2" WRITTEN BY HEAD PRO MARK JOHNS ESPECIALLY FOR YOU.

A PHOTON PHOTO WORKS THE BEST

A PHOTON IN THE VECTOR CIRCUMFERENCE IS A SURE THING WHEN IT COMES TO ADDRESSING

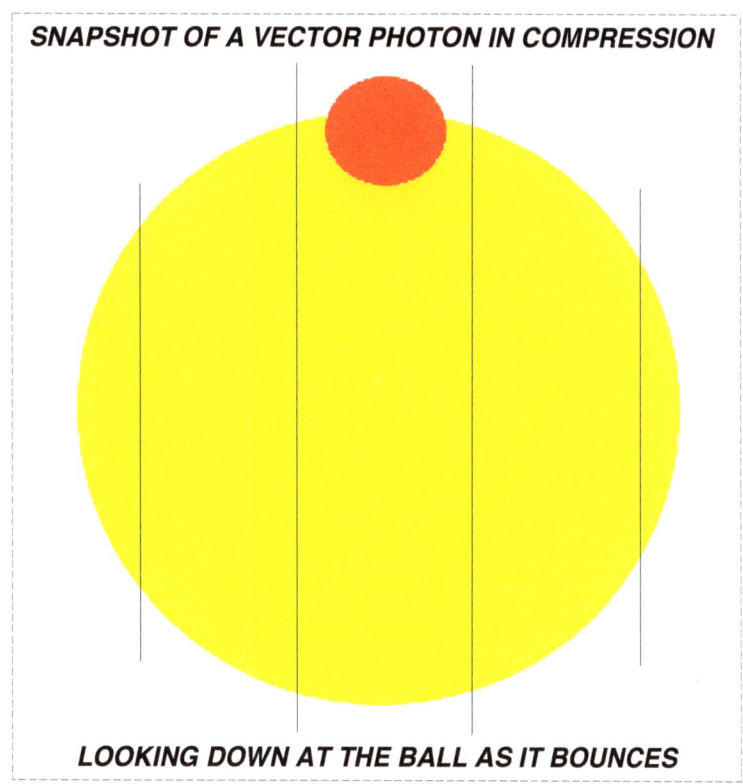

SNAPSHOT OF A VECTOR PHOTON IN COMPRESSION

LOOKING DOWN AT THE BALL AS IT BOUNCES

After you vortex the opponent's impact, prepare to "vectorize" the ball in compression. Capturing the vector address as the ball bounces may seem to be a difficult task, but this is not the case. It is really quite easy and is accomplished by simply seeing for the ball's front circumference for as little as a few milliseconds. Once this address is seen the physical response will be generated by it's accompanying information. This information is critical for developing the timing of your swing and is used by the subconscious for responding physically. While viewing the circumference any address can be converted into a photon by asking the question "what" and the correct address will light up.

You maybe doubtful about the existence of a photon address.

⬅ *tennis king "physics"* ➡

This is simply emotional resistance to the elevated mental concept of mind over matter.

TENNIS KING EQUATION^2 "BEYOND THE VORTEX"
OPTIMAL PLAY THROUGH "ENERGY FIELD" RECOGNITION

The "vertorization" of a ball's address is the way we get to see the photon. The ball's bounce is .008 milliseconds long and if we only catch a photon address for .001 milliseconds - you have enough information to hit successfully.

The thing to remember is to hold the image of this "photon photo" once it is recorded by the consciousness throughout the hitting of the ball. The player must not try to hit the ball or even see the ball after you have taken your "photon photo".

Take your photo and forget the ball till it comes out of your impact.

TENNIS KING EQUATION ^{2} "BEYOND THE VORTEX"
OPTIMAL PLAY THROUGH "ENERGY FIELD" RECOGNITION

"TENNIS KING EQUATION 2" WRITTEN BY HEAD PRO MARK JOHNS ESPECIALLY FOR YOU.

"THERE CAN BE ONLY ONE"

SHOT SELECTION IS NOT A CONSCIOUS FUNCTION - THE OPTIMAL ADDRESS IS DETERMINED THE BALL.

"I could have hit the ball cross court or down the line and what did I do - I missed the shot all together."

Every player has experienced this situation and shutters to think of how the match might of turned out if they had done it differently. The way to success is certainly a different perspective, but it is not about what shot you select. It is about the state of mind used to generate the "shot selection"

A SERIES OF A VECTOR ADDRESSES & ONE PHOTON

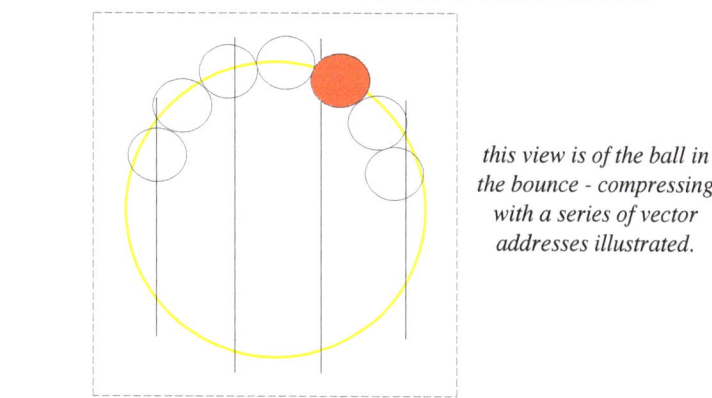

this view is of the ball in the bounce - compressing with a series of vector addresses illustrated.

LOOKING DOWN ASK THE BALL "WHAT" ADDRESS?

Shot selection is not a conscious mind function. Once the conscious mind ponders which shot to hit the "ball orientation" is lost and the unforced error occurs. Ask the ball for the vector address and shot selection becomes a by product of the ball orientation and shot materializes subconsciously.

Shot selection is found in the ball not the conscious mind.
⬅ **tennis king "physics"** ➡
The number of possibilities confuses the conscious mind - so avoid them altogether.

TENNIS KING EQUATION ^{2} "BEYOND THE VORTEX"
OPTIMAL PLAY THROUGH "ENERGY FIELD" RECOGNITION

The idea that "shot selection" is not a conscious minded process is surely a debatable concept for many players. The only way to resolve the dilemma of where "shot selection" comes from - either the conscious mind or ball orientation - is to allow the flow of information the ball is sending your way to create your response.

To experience this flow of information all you need do is vortex the opponent's impact and then watch the ball descend into the bounce. Your focus "sight-line" will run along the ball's vector till an address shows up. Don't worry - you will recognize the address when you see it. When it does take a snapshot of it and your work is done.

Trust the ball to manage all the variables of the playing field.

TENNIS KING EQUATION ^{2} "BEYOND THE VORTEX"
OPTIMAL PLAY THROUGH "ENERGY FIELD" RECOGNITION

"TENNIS KING EQUATION 2" WRITTEN BY HEAD PRO MARK JOHNS ESPECIALLY FOR YOU.

"MAKING TIME STAND STILL"

SEARCHING FOR DETAILS MANUFACTURES TIME TO THE POINT OF ENDLESSNESS.

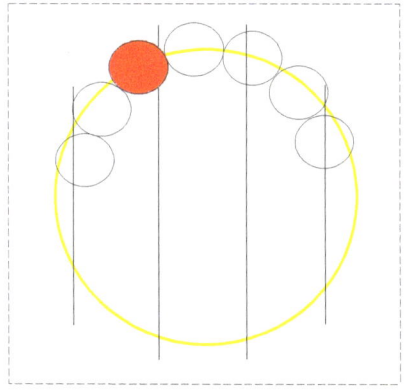

A VIEW OF THE VECTOR ADDRESS

This illustration is of a captured photon address on the ball's vector during the bounce. It is ready and waiting for you to take your snap shot.

Before you take your snapshot pour as much focus intensity into the sight-line as you can. By doing this you will create the feeling that time is standing still.

A VIEW OF A PHOTON EXPLODED

The result of this tremendous focused energy will be the explosion of the photon address. When a photon exploded it is magnified to the point that you are aware of nothing else.

It will become the only thing your focus will allow you to see. This exclusive view blocks any conscious effort to hit the ball. By seeking this ultimate level of detail you have seemly stopped time and making the physical response a sure thing

The explosion of a photon address produces the sensation that time has stopped.

⬅ *tennis king "physics"* ➡

The ability to explodes the photon is found it the exclusively intense focus on the vector.

TENNIS KING EQUATION ^{2} "BEYOND THE VORTEX"
OPTIMAL PLAY THROUGH "ENERGY FIELD" RECOGNITION

The misuse of time is the underlying cause for failure. We all start the match with enough time to hit the shots and win the points. When we fail to hit the shot, we incorrectly think the cause for failure is something physical or strategical. The true cause lies in the fabric of time. What this means is how time is perceived and experienced by the player. This perception determines the environment in which the player resides and competes in.

The Tibetan monk slows his heart down to the point that it almost stops. This is the result of a specific function of mind. The tennis player can do the same thing to the ball. By using a highly charged and focused "sight-line" to view a future dimension of time, the physical response is insulated from distraction.

To stop time and see the future all you have do is explode the vector photon address.

TENNIS KING EQUATION ^{2} "BEYOND THE VORTEX"
OPTIMAL PLAY THROUGH "ENERGY FIELD" RECOGNITION

"TENNIS KING EQUATION 2" WRITTEN BY HEAD PRO MARK JOHNS ESPECIALLY FOR YOU.

3

"TIME AND SPACE"

TENNIS KING EQUATION² "BEYOND THE VORTEX"
OPTIMAL PLAY THROUGH "ENERGY FIELD" RECOGNITION

The Tennis King terminology:

time and space = the expansion of time is constant. It leaves in it's wake physical space.

time dilation = the expandition of a moment to the point where time slows down and details increase.

alpha and beta states = 2 states of mind measured by brain wave activity.

quantum scalar dynamics = the detection of visual and temporal references to access future dimensions of time through your focus sight-lines.

crossovers = a mental error the produces physical mistakes. The player drops the mental vector address and tries to hit the physical ball.

oksom = the "ok state of mind'. This allows the player to play without mental negativity.

"TENNIS KING EQUATION 2" WRITTEN BY HEAD PRO MARK JOHNS ESPECIALLY FOR YOU.

UNDERSTANDING "TIME OVER SPACE" PARADIGM

GAIN THE ADVANTAGE BY USING TIME TO CONQUER SPACE.

The "time over space" equation is shown by seeing a player swinging down into the ball at the bounce.

The player's sight-line is directed into the ball's vector as it compresses, establishing an address which triggers the swing.

A player trying to hit the ball after the bounce is trapped in the dimension of "space". Observe the blue swing and the yellow ball trajectories.

Combined they represent twice the time and effort as a player in the dimesion of "time".

The player with a mind in "time" always beats the player with a mind in "space".

⬅——— ***tennis king "physics"*** ———➡

Anybody can be programmed to play in the dimension of "time".

TENNIS KING EQUATION² "BEYOND THE VORTEX"
OPTIMAL PLAY THROUGH "ENERGY FIELD" RECOGNITION

A simple diagram like this one shows you the advantage of "time over space". Players are taught and conditioned inadvertently to be rooted into "space" right from the beginning of their sports careers. Trying to hit the ball at the impact seems like the right thing to do. It is not the best way or the easiest.

Anybody can be trained to play in the dimension of "time". They only need to understand that it is to their advantage to learn it and it it will quickly replace all of the "space" references that now motorize the physical responses.

To be a player of "time" one need only believe and it will occur.

TENNIS KING EQUATION ^{2} "BEYOND THE VORTEX"
OPTIMAL PLAY THROUGH "ENERGY FIELD" RECOGNITION

"TENNIS KING EQUATION 2" WRITTEN BY HEAD PRO MARK JOHNS ESPECIALLY FOR YOU.

FIND THE BLACK HOLE ON LEVELS 4 & 5

OF THE FIVE STATES OF MIND - THE BLACK HOLE RESIDES ON DEEPEST LEVELS

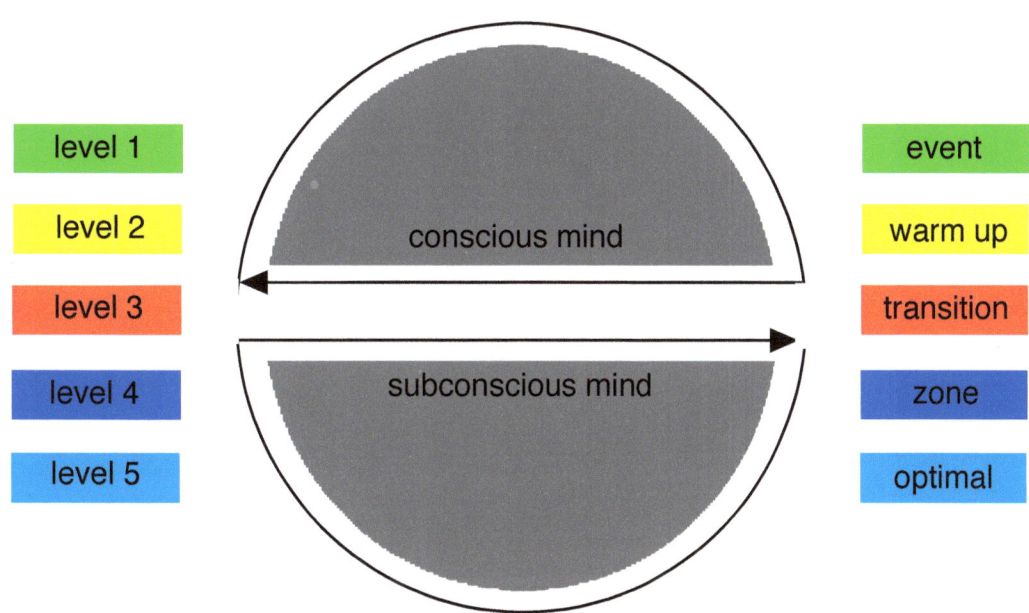

The player moves through several states of mind during the course of a match. The Tennis King Equation breaks them into five distinct levels in order for a player to be able to maneuver from one state of mind to the next.

1. The "event" level. This is defined as a physical awareness of the court, the opponent and any surrounding characteristics. 2. The "warm up". This is the player's awareness of his body, the strokes and the ball. 3. The "transition" from the "self orientation" into the "ball orientation". Player begins to see details on the ball while losing self awareness. 4. The "zone" defined by complete ball awareness including vortex and vector references that move the player from the dimension of "space" into the dimension of "time". 5. The "optimal" state is the recognition of the force fields that move the ball before the actual physical event.

The mind exsists on many levels and the player can move between them at will.

tennis king "physics"

The state of mind corralates directly to a specific dimension of time or space.

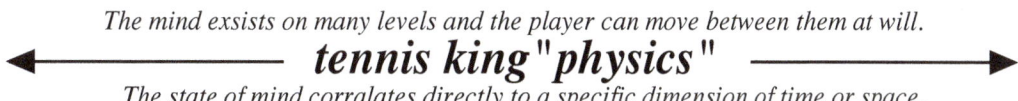

Now more than ever the player relates the state of mind as the source for the level of physical performance. Working on the mind is the way we change the physical play. Each level of mind represents certain physical aspects in our performance potential.

The player's performance is a mental exercise of intellectual and emotional manipulation. We can become experts in mind control with constant practice.

Eventually we realize the performance is equal to our mental discipline.

TENNIS KING EQUATION^2 "BEYOND THE VORTEX"
OPTIMAL PLAY THROUGH "ENERGY FIELD" RECOGNITION

"TENNIS KING EQUATION 2" WRITTEN BY HEAD PRO MARK JOHNS ESPECIALLY FOR YOU.

CONSCIOUS COMPOSITION

THE EMOTIONAL BALANCE IS DETERMINED BY WHERE YOUR FOCUS IS.

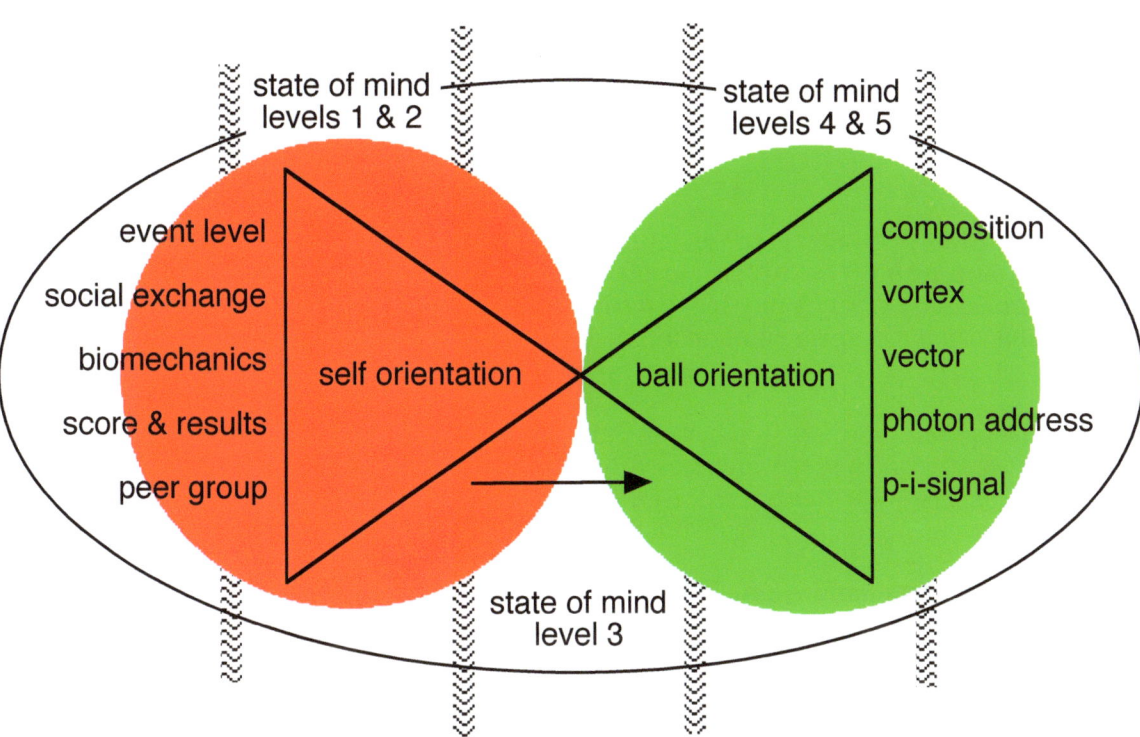

Emotional balance is the key factor in managing the player's energy expenditure during a match. The player who plays from state of mind (s.o.m.) level of 1 or 2 is going to experience a lot more emotional stress then a player in level 4 or 5. This stress is going to distract the player from progressing to higher levels of recognition that are available on levels 4 and 5. This is obviously going to result in lower performance of play levels.

The player can create the s.o.m. transformation by leaving conscious mind event level references like social exchanges, biomechanics, score and peer group considerations behind and pick the ball orientation - composition level references. The vortex and vector, a photon address and the post impact signal will move you into s.o.m. levels 4 and 5 while simultaneously moving you out of physical space and into 1st dimension of time.

The emotional energy of the mind is the power source for the player.

⬅ *tennis king "physics"* ➡

How you manage this power determines the range of the performance potential.

TENNIS KING EQUATION² "BEYOND THE VORTEX"
OPTIMAL PLAY THROUGH "ENERGY FIELD" RECOGNITION

The flow of emotion is the dictating factor behind the flow on energy in the physical realm. The two or four player's states of mind driven by emotional power actually create a physical landscape of the match. The player who knows this can build up an emotional momentum that transforms into a superior physical response.

The progressive development of emotional strength assures the player of eventual success in the awareness of the force fields at work and how to respond to them. The force fields and the emotional fields are one and the same "field" when there is no intervening distraction to create a fragmentation and confusion.

Build a secure emotional foundation and observe your progress.

TENNIS KING EQUATION ^{2} "BEYOND THE VORTEX"
OPTIMAL PLAY THROUGH "ENERGY FIELD" RECOGNITION

"TENNIS KING EQUATION 2" WRITTEN BY HEAD PRO MARK JOHNS ESPECIALLY FOR YOU.

THE MULTI VERSE IS HERE & NOW & WHEN

WITH 11 DIMENSIONS OF TIME TO WORK FROM - YOU WILL NEVER BE BORED

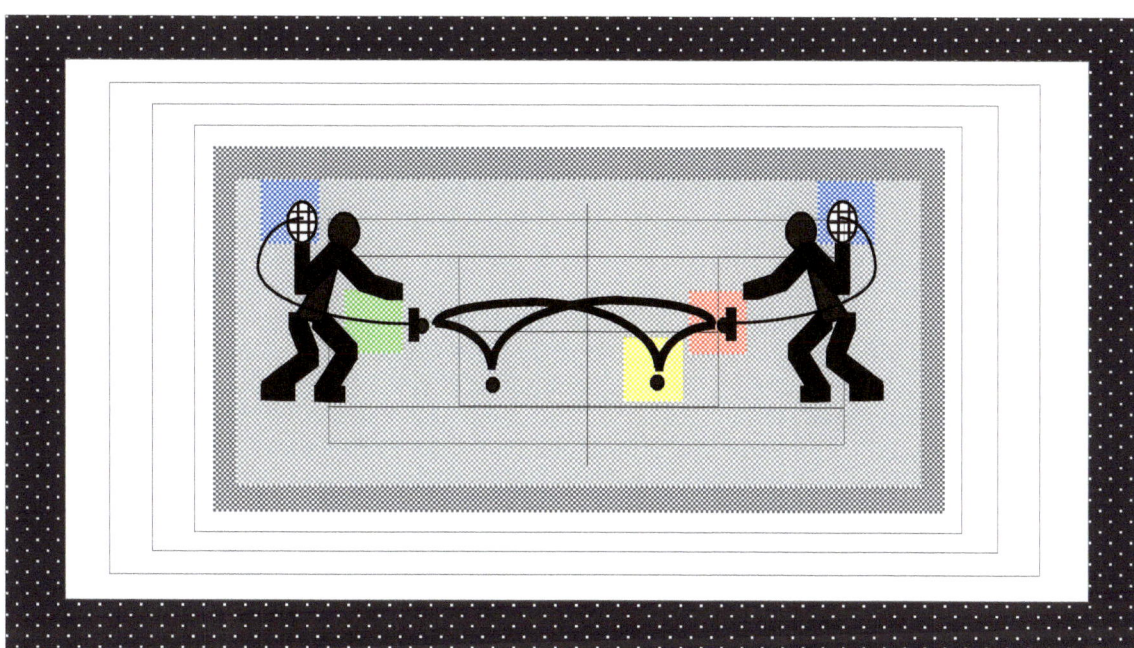

Eleven dimensions of time? - oh my!

The world of quantum "anything" is a strange place - quantum physics is even stranger. The "string theory" allows for at least 11 separate time frames - a multi verse of realities. As a player which one do you reside? Which one is the right one or the better one? Now that is a very good question. This diagram is my tennis reality. The red box (0) is physical space - this is the ball as you make contact. The yellow box (1) is the first dimension of time located in the compression of the bounce. Green (2) is the opponent's vortex bridge - blue (3) is the time tunnel on the opponent's racket face. The time dimensions (4-10) are transcending levels of information and understandings that players intuitively realize as they relax and integrate into time. The black box (11) as you may guessed is a blackhole - time at a standstill.

Have you ever experienced the sensation of time stopping?

Eleven dimensions of time leaves alot of room for improvement.

⬅ ——— *tennis king "physics"* ——— ➡

As a player moves upward in time frames the physical world is easier to negotiate.

TENNIS KING EQUATION² "BEYOND THE VORTEX"
OPTIMAL PLAY THROUGH "ENERGY FIELD" RECOGNITION

Just think about it for a moment. The construction of reality is layered. The more layers you realize the greater your experience. When watching first round play of a tournament it may seem like the players are really great. Who could possibly beat them? Then they lose in the next round - what happened - physically they looked unbeatable. Millions of players around the world are rated by which level of time their game resides in.

That really great player loses in the second round because he just met a player residing in a higher level in time.

All good players know what to do - the better players knows "when" to do it.

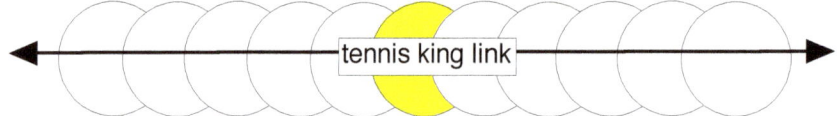

TENNIS KING EQUATION ^{2} "BEYOND THE VORTEX"
OPTIMAL PLAY THROUGH "ENERGY FIELD" RECOGNITION

"TENNIS KING EQUATION 2" WRITTEN BY HEAD PRO MARK JOHNS ESPECIALLY FOR YOU.

PERCEPTION OF TIME EQUALS THE STATE OF MIND

YOU CAN MOVE INTO A BETTER FRAME OF MIND BY SLOWING DOWN TIME

THE MOTION OF TIME IS CONSTANT - BUT...

it is not uniform. The law of relativity allows for time to be perceived at varying rates. This is demonstrated in Einstein's "twin's paradox". This is where one twin remains on earth and the other travels through space in a rocket at near the speed of light. After 10 years of space travel the one twin returns to earth and finds his brother has long since passed away and many decades have passed. Time is a commodity that can be manipulated mentally and with practice the manipulation of time can manipulate the state of mind. By getting out of ourselves and by getting into the manipulation of time, we are able to move into optimal states of mind relevant to our surroundings.

THE TENNIS KING EQUATION "TIME DILATION" METHOD

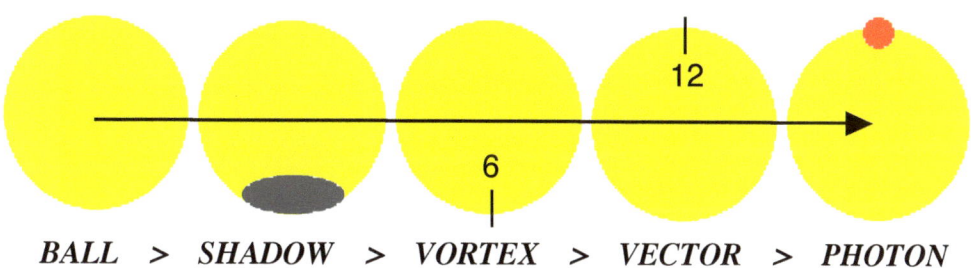

BALL > SHADOW > VORTEX > VECTOR > PHOTON

The way to change our perception of time is to start out by seeing a greater number of details in the physical space. Once a "detail orientation" is established the mind begins to emotionally stabilize. The next step is to refine the number of details to the ones that are critical to the intended function. Once these essential references are recognized, start to create a new and intensified level of focus to clarify details in these details. This entire process is going to change your perception of time and as time transforms - so does your state of mind.

In "life and death" situations time may seem to slow down time.

◄──────────── *tennis king "physics"* ────────────►

The further we integrate into the visual details the more we synchronize into time.

TENNIS KING EQUATION² "BEYOND THE VORTEX"
OPTIMAL PLAY THROUGH "ENERGY FIELD" RECOGNITION

The concept of "time dilation" is based on the player's ability to expand the moment. The prolongation of a specific moment allows the player more time to develop a recognition of the "detail orientation". The perception of this extended time frame by the player will be that time has slowed down.

The idea that time is moving slower will allow the player to feel more confident that he or she will be able to perform whatever function that is necessary in the moment. Remember most errors are created when a player feels rushed by a shortage of time.

Controlling the passage of time will also create a sense of security.

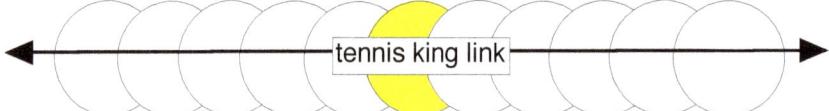

"TENNIS KING EQUATION 2" WRITTEN BY HEAD PRO MARK JOHNS ESPECIALLY FOR YOU.

SYNCHRONIZATION OF THE WAVES

ALLOWING THE ENTRAINMENT OF YOUR BRAIN WAVES TO THE PHYSICAL FIELD IS KEY.

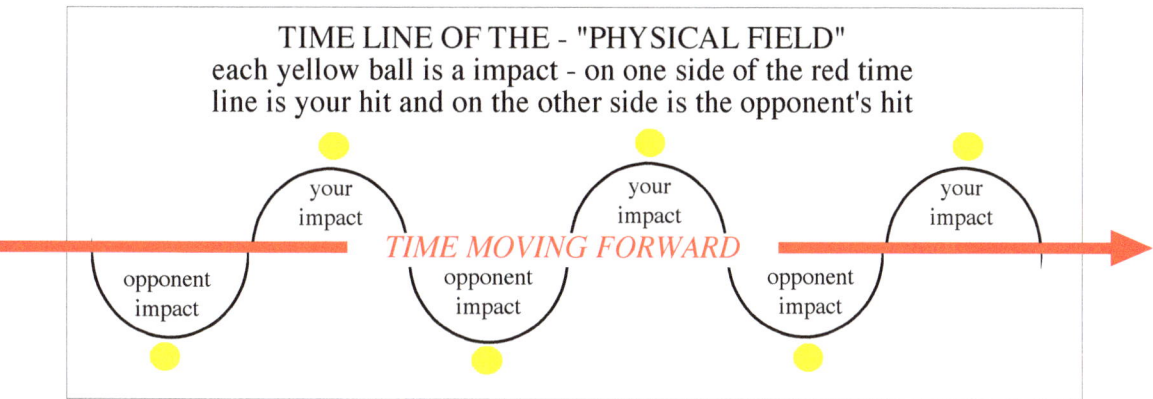

The energy field is defined by all energetic systems residing in a particular environment. In tennis this field will include the all the physical features - the court, balls, rackets, weather, lighting and the players. The player who can simulate a matching mental energy to the physical field will be in synch with the action and his physical play will be generated by this. The player can entrain his brain waves to the physical realm by defining the vortex and vector for each impact.

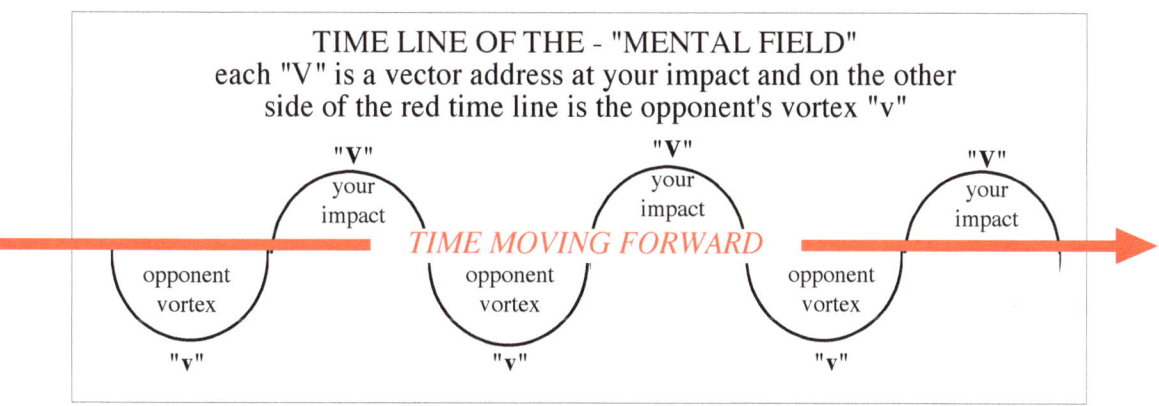

Losing self awareness allows for total energy field awareness.

← tennis king *"physics"* →

The details in the ball orientation can be used to delete self awareness

TENNIS KING EQUATION^2 "BEYOND THE VORTEX"

OPTIMAL PLAY THROUGH "ENERGY FIELD" RECOGNITION

The energy field is moving forward with the motion of time. All the components in the field are carried along in either a state of harmony or discord. Players are going to move through the course of a match in varying degrees of both with the winner being the one that spends more of the time in synch with the action than not.

Going with the flow of energy becomes much easier as you integrate deeper into the details of the ball orientation. Programming your mind to seek specific references relevant to the flow of energy is the name of the game.

Establish your sequence of details to flow forward effortlessly.

TENNIS KING EQUATION ^{2} "BEYOND THE VORTEX"
OPTIMAL PLAY THROUGH "ENERGY FIELD" RECOGNITION

"TENNIS KING EQUATION 2" WRITTEN BY HEAD PRO MARK JOHNS ESPECIALLY FOR YOU.

THE SPECTRUM OF FOCUS INSTENSITY

YOUR SIGHT-LINES REQUIRE VARYING FREQUENCIES OF ENERGY TO GET THE JOB DONE

Like the spectrums of light or sound the focus spectrum is based on the intensity of energy or the energy's frequency . A light chart of visible colors defines this spectrum of frequencies from 400 nanometers (low wavelength) for violet to 700 nm (high wavelength) for red. Using this correlation of "colors to focus" you can realize different frequencies of mental energies to create your sight-lines.

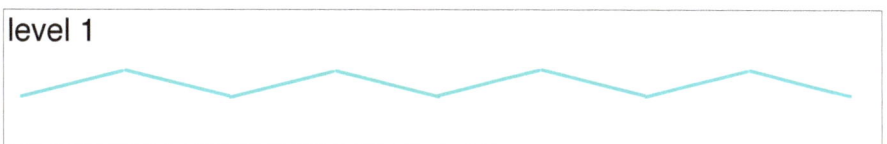

Level 1 sight-line is a low frequency focus. A soft energy is used to address the ball in warm up & soft angle shots, drop shots, volleys.

Level 2 sight-line is a stronger frequency focus. This higher frequency is effective for producing ground strokes during baseline rallies.

Level 3 sight-line is a intense focus. This high frequency sight-line is used less often. It is used to hit winners, serve returns & approaches.

Level 4 sight-line is a super focus. This highest frequency sight-line is used for extremely stressful situations like break & match points.

The focus energy is the composition of the sight-lines that direct the physical response

⬅ ─── *tennis king "physics"* ─── ➡

Manipulating of focus creates a full range shots for varying circumstances.

TENNIS KING EQUATION^2 "BEYOND THE VORTEX"
OPTIMAL PLAY THROUGH "ENERGY FIELD" RECOGNITION

Music is the composition of sounds that fit together in a sequential order to create a harmony. When the listener hears a missed note - it is a note that doesn't fit properly into the sequence. This note has a frequency that is dissimilar to the the others. It may be to high or to low, but it is definitely noticeable.

The frequency of any form of energy fluctuates within a prescribed spectrum. This is critical information for the tennis player because it allows a manipulation of calculated energy to create a spectrum of physical responses.

The customization of focus sight-lines means that the player can adjust the frequency of the focus through the mental application of emotion energy compatible to the momentary circumstances.

To hit harder one does not swing harder - the player only needs to focus harder.

TENNIS KING EQUATION^2 "BEYOND THE VORTEX"
OPTIMAL PLAY THROUGH "ENERGY FIELD" RECOGNITION

"TENNIS KING EQUATION 2" WRITTEN BY HEAD PRO MARK JOHNS ESPECIALLY FOR YOU.

DON'T TOUCH THE SNAKE !

TRYING TO HIT THE BALL IS LIKE TOUCHING THE SNAKE - IT CAN BE VERY DANGEROUS

The snake analogy is very interesting because 99% of all tennis players think that they need to try to hit the ball. The ball will hit itself if you just watch it properly.

TENNIS KING MOTTO:

"LOOK- BUT DON'T TOUCH !"

How does this concept work? The "ball hitting itself" is a "catch phrase" for a powerful and critical function of the subconscious replying to stimuli. This common matrix of shared energy between the ball and subconscious maybe the difficult to accept and could possibly be the greatest obstacle in a player's development. It may require years for a player to experience this relationship and yet still not understand what it is.

Trying to hit the ball is a conscious effort which will block the incoming information from the ball because the player's focus has switched from the ball to the physical swing. This resulting gap of information represents the error about to occur.

On the other hand, the player producing a focus that continually absorbs the ball's data is assured to hit that ball without any conscious awareness of the swing that does not fail.

The player must trust his "hand to eye coordination" to hit the ball.

⬅ *tennis king "physics"* ➡

The sooner a player realizes that the body follows the mind the better.

TENNIS KING EQUATION² "BEYOND THE VORTEX"
OPTIMAL PLAY THROUGH "ENERGY FIELD" RECOGNITION

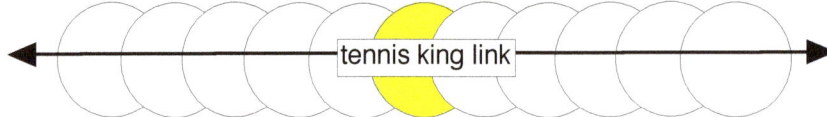

We do it all it all the time. Trusting our subconscious to tend to the details. Examples of this are easy to recognize, we drive our cars and talk to our passengers simultaneously without losing control of the physical realm.

Hitting a tennis ball is as easy as turning on a light switch. We needn't think about our technique for turning on the lights, so why do we consider the proper technique for hitting the ball. When we do errors occur.

The reason hitting the ball can be a simple task is that the visual perspective is constantly updating our motor cortex with the relevant information so it can create the best physical response.

When hitting the ball -the focus is on the ball - not the swing.

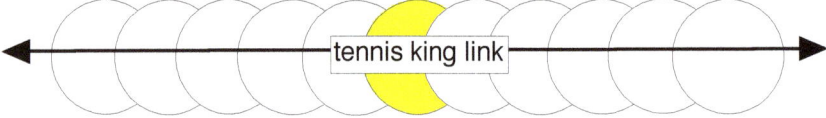

"TENNIS KING EQUATION 2" WRITTEN BY HEAD PRO MARK JOHNS ESPECIALLY FOR YOU.

QUANTUM SCALAR DYNAMICS

YOU CAN "SCALAR" BY ESTABLISHING TIME LINE REFERENCES!

The Tennis King Scalar Focus Wave

The "scalar focus" is a series of sight lines that penetrate your opponent's impact and define specific events in time. This wave of observation will result in the generation of the physical response. The time line above is seen left to right. The abbreviations "dot" = dimensions in time and "dos" = space.

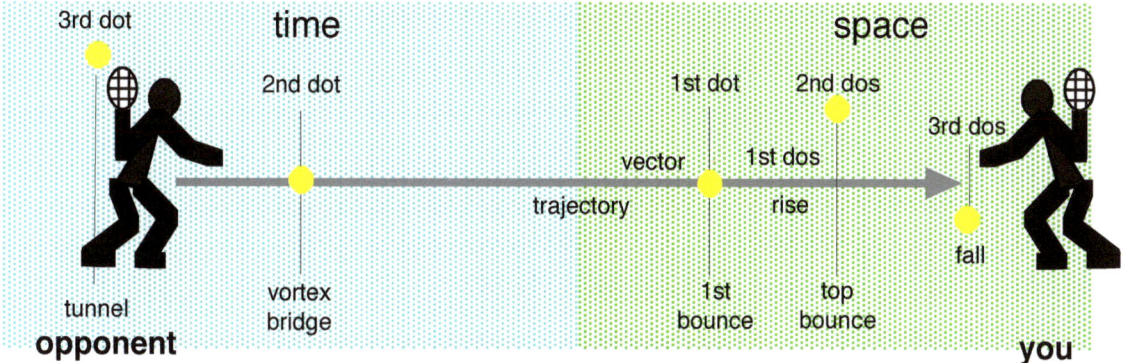

the time dimensions

3rd dot = the tunnel - the earliest visual - located before the bridge.
2nd dot = the bridge - space between the ball and opponent's racket.
1st dot = the vector - located on ball circumference during the bounce.

the space dimensions

1st dos = the ball coming out of the bounce.
2nd dos = the ball at the top of the bounce.
3rd dos = the ball dropping off the top of the bounce.

Mind over matter = time over space

Depending on when and where your informations is coming from determines how well you are playing. The freshest info comes from deep in time is aquired with a scalar focus. The player responding to late in "space" info will always go down the the "scalar player".

The conscious mind is limited to the number of references it can handle.

⬅ *tennis king "physics"* ➡

When the scalar focus wave function is employed the response is from the subconscious.

TENNIS KING EQUATION² "BEYOND THE VORTEX"
OPTIMAL PLAY THROUGH "ENERGY FIELD" RECOGNITION

Where is your game heading? Are you focusing on physical improvements in your stroke production? Is this your idea or your instructor's idea as to how you will increase performance? If so - I have only one comment for you.

Forget about it !

You need to place all your energy into developing your mental game. The physical game follows the mental game as in "form follows function".

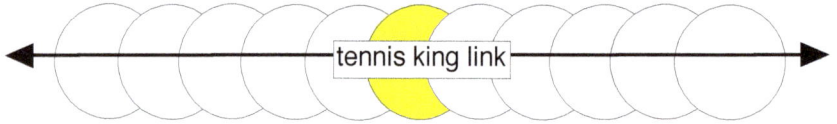

TENNIS KING EQUATION ^{2} "BEYOND THE VORTEX"
OPTIMAL PLAY THROUGH "ENERGY FIELD" RECOGNITION

"TENNIS KING EQUATION 2" WRITTEN BY HEAD PRO MARK JOHNS ESPECIALLY FOR YOU.

THE VORTEX AXIS IS THE "BRIDGE" INTO THE FUTURE

THE VORTEX IS THE "DNA" OF THE SHOT YET TO BE HIT.

The vortex axis is the center line between the racket and the ball. It is the precursor of all actions that will influence the ball in the soon to follow physical dimension. It is like the *"DNA"* of the unborn shot. The player that can isolate this vortex axis is totally informed to what shot is coming and where and how to respond to it.

The key to acquiring this information is to vortex the opponent's impact by observing the declining space between the ball and the racket.

The speed of the closing of the vortex is the first clue to capturing the "axis".

Once you have been able to realize how fast the vortex is closing down you will be able to define the time frame of the up coming shot. This will lead you to seeing other shot characteristics like the spin and angle. The vortex axis contains all the information you need to respond to the shot.

vortex

vortex axis is a visual bridge

The time spent "vortexing" is not taking away from the response time.

⟵ *tennis king "physics"* ⟶

It is actually giving you the time line of the event and allowing you to use it correctly.

TENNIS KING EQUATION² "BEYOND THE VORTEX"
OPTIMAL PLAY THROUGH "ENERGY FIELD" RECOGNITION

The "Tennis King Equation" is represented on the physical level by the opponent's impact (the vortex) and your impact (the vector). They are the windows we look through to access the dimension of time. The ability to see a vortex or vector is a skill that can be developed and refined to the end result equaling a better physical game.

The time frame in which a tennis point exists is hinged on the vortex and the vector. Each is of equal importance and combined together are all the information being offered to the player from which a reply of a compatible nature is generated.

The idea of "time over space" is a result of vortex and vector information.

TENNIS KING EQUATION^2 "BEYOND THE VORTEX"
OPTIMAL PLAY THROUGH "ENERGY FIELD" RECOGNITION

"TENNIS KING EQUATION 2" WRITTEN BY HEAD PRO MARK JOHNS ESPECIALLY FOR YOU.

TAKE THE ALPHA-BETA TIME TUNNEL

USE THE "ALPHA WEDGE" FOCUS TECHNIQUE TO MOVE FORWARD THROUGH THE CONES OF TIME

All the action is happening in the "cones of time". The "alpha cone" is a pre-impact triangle of time where the bridge exsists and the "beta cone" is a post impact where your physical response resides.

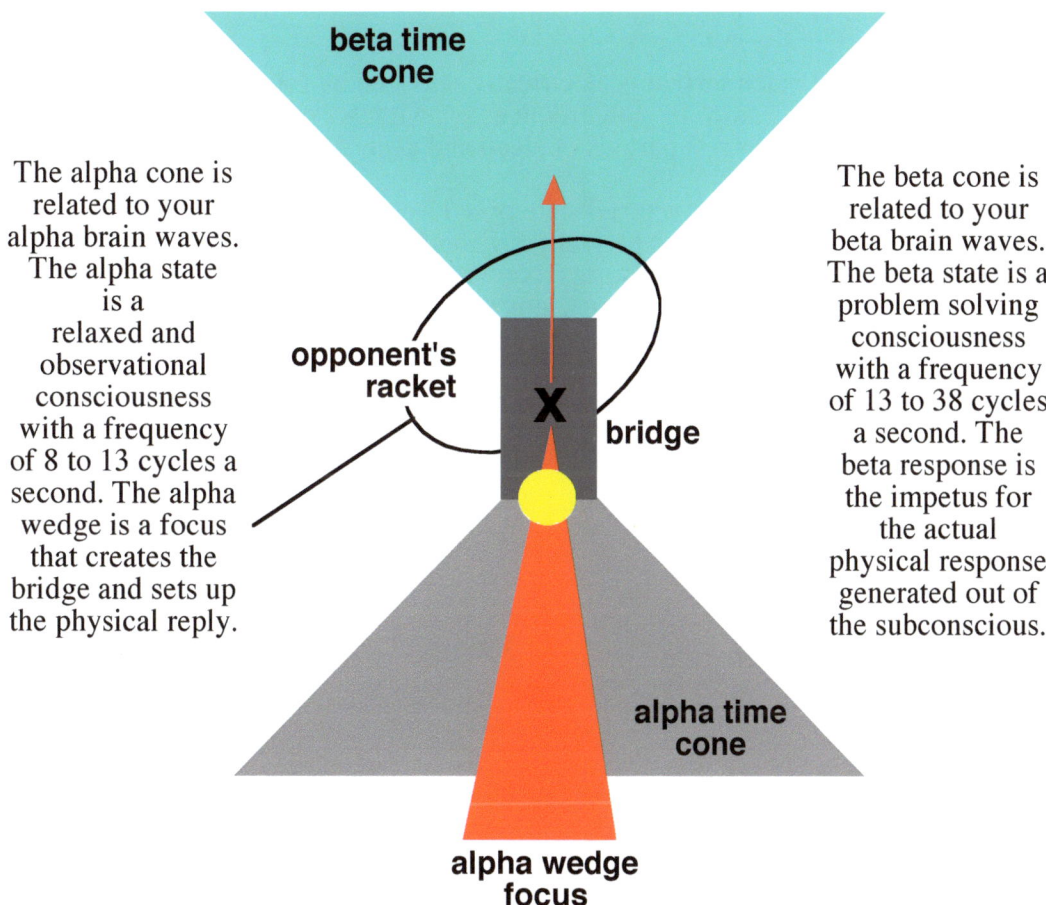

The alpha cone is related to your alpha brain waves. The alpha state is a relaxed and observational consciousness with a frequency of 8 to 13 cycles a second. The alpha wedge is a focus that creates the bridge and sets up the physical reply.

The beta cone is related to your beta brain waves. The beta state is a problem solving consciousness with a frequency of 13 to 38 cycles a second. The beta response is the impetus for the actual physical response generated out of the subconscious.

Creating an alpha beta focus begins with the "alpha wedge".

tennis king "physics"

The shift from the "alpha state" to the "beta state" in the mind is automatic

TENNIS KING EQUATION^2 "BEYOND THE VORTEX"
OPTIMAL PLAY THROUGH "ENERGY FIELD" RECOGNITION

The mind is a balanced machine that is electrically powered by four basic brain waves. The "delta and the theta" are very slow frequencies, with 4-7 cycles a second. They represent our rest periods of sleep and deep relaxation.

The "alpha wave" is a wakeful and relaxed state of 8-13 cycles, that produces a very calm and observant consciousness. This is perfect for visualizing the vortex bridge and scalar bar. The "beta wave" is more business like with 13-38 cycles a second. This consciousness is the trigger for the subconscious physical response. The revolving cycle of the "alpha-beta" combo is the basis of the "scalar" focus wave.

The "scalar" focus is how you can "see it early & hit it hard."

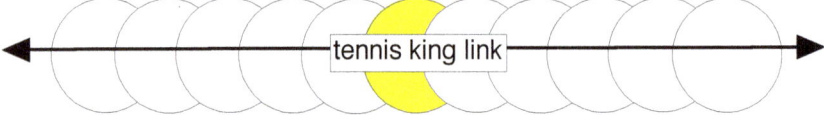

TENNIS KING EQUATION ^{2} "BEYOND THE VORTEX"
OPTIMAL PLAY THROUGH "ENERGY FIELD" RECOGNITION

"TENNIS KING EQUATION 2" WRITTEN BY HEAD PRO MARK JOHNS ESPECIALLY FOR YOU.

CROSSOVERS AND ANOREADERS

THE MOST COMMON ERRORS IN THE WORLD OF QUANTUM SCALAR DYNAMICS

The crossover is a mental error that occurs when a player's conscious mind perceives the bridge and sees the scalar bar. Then just before impact the conscious mind stops holding the mental imagery of the bridge and the bar and switches to another image. This mental "crossover" most often is to the physical awareness of hitting the ball. The substitution from the bridge and bar (representing the ball orientation) to the physical swing (self orientation) will cause enough loss of ball information uptake to cause an unforced error.

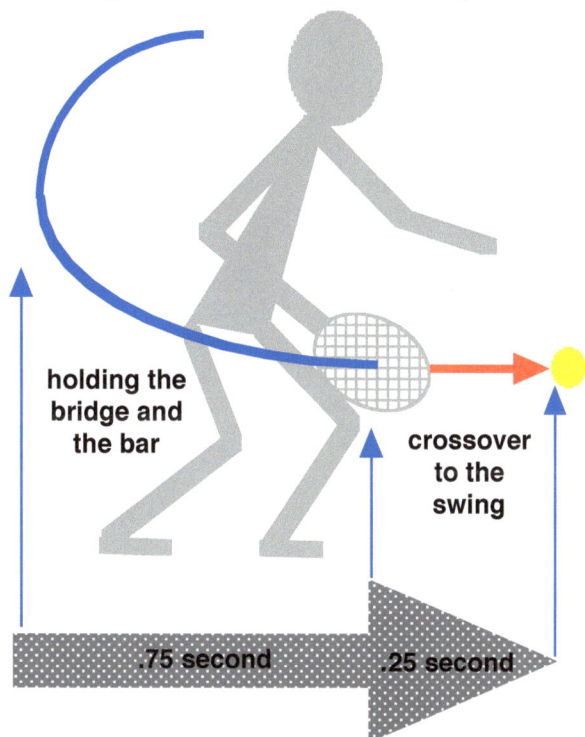

The anoreader (a no reader) is another cause for unforced errors. The "anoreader" is the misreading of the opponent's bridge. Some players can hold off to the last millisecond before revealing the true bridge of their shot. This can cause a premature expectation which misleads you into thinking in one direction and the ball going off in the other.

The reason why tennis is a mental game is because everthing happens in the mind first.

◄──────── *tennis king "physics"* ────────►

A calm objective state of mind make far less errors than the chaotic mind.

TENNIS KING EQUATION ² "BEYOND THE VORTEX"
OPTIMAL PLAY THROUGH "ENERGY FIELD" RECOGNITION

The player is subjected to all kinds of stress. Stress is the foundation of distraction. The physical, intellectual, and the emotional realms are where stress does it damage.

Physical stress can be seen in the fitness and coordination components. A player who tires faster or is slower than the opponent feels greater physical stress.

Intellectual stress is based on the player's knowledge. A player who knows less about the composition of tennis will encounter greater stress than a more knowledgeable opponent

Emotional stress is the most critical - it is a compound of the other two stresses.

TENNIS KING EQUATION ^{2} "BEYOND THE VORTEX"
OPTIMAL PLAY THROUGH "ENERGY FIELD" RECOGNITION

"TENNIS KING EQUATION 2" WRITTEN BY HEAD PRO MARK JOHNS ESPECIALLY FOR YOU.

ON THE "WALL OF TIME"

TAKING YOUR 3-D PERSPECTIVE OF THE OPPONENT'S IMPACT AND CONVERTING IT TO ONE DIMENSION

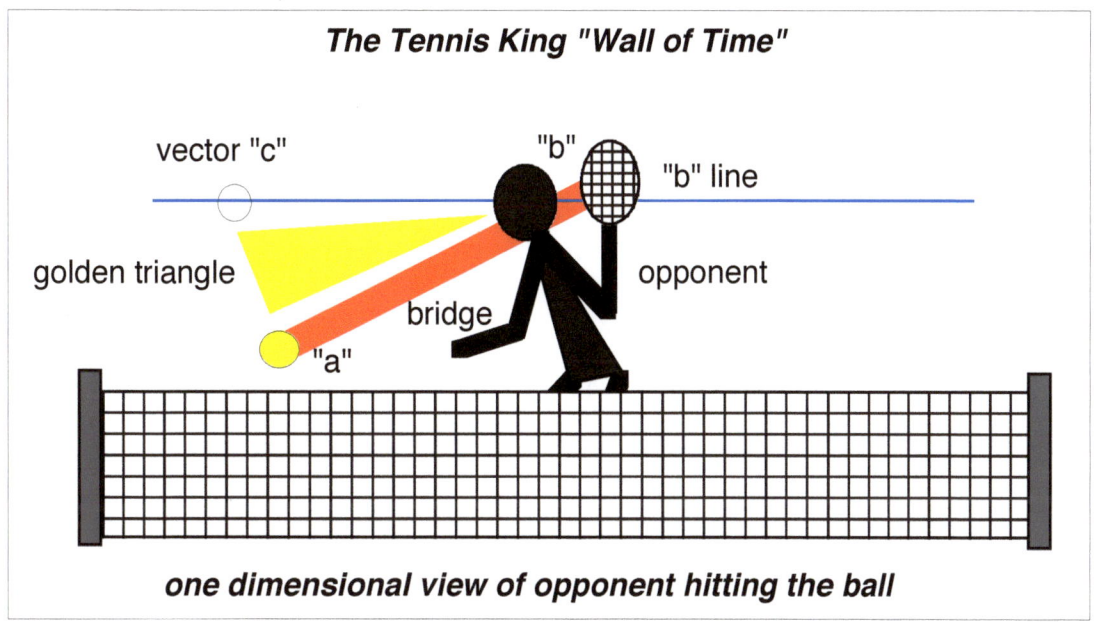

The diagram above of the "wall of time" is in one dimensional because it exists on the printed page. We automatically see it as a three dimensional illustration in our mind by inserting the depth perspective to make it understandable. This creates a multitude of variables that slow down our physical response, because we attempt to interpret what they represent before we act.

Take the view of your opponent hitting the ball and mentally convert it into a one dimensional perspective. The "bridge" and vector "c" will be easily implemented on this flat screen. The result is a much faster response time, so you can hit the ball much earlier.

The conscious mind wants to complicate things to create greater understandings.

⬅ ——— *tennis king "physics"* ——— ➡

The subconscious mind doesn't need anything but the timing to generate response.

TENNIS KING EQUATION² "BEYOND THE VORTEX"
OPTIMAL PLAY THROUGH "ENERGY FIELD" RECOGNITION

The way we see the world can be adjusted for specific purposes. The tennis player wants to simplifiy the response sequence to as few visual references as possible.

The "wall of time" is a one dimensional view of the playing field that alows us to process infomation rapidly and respond quicker then if you see the usual three dimensional perspective. This also reduces emotinal stress because it is less complex.

The "Wall of Time" is all four dimensions of reality rolled into one.

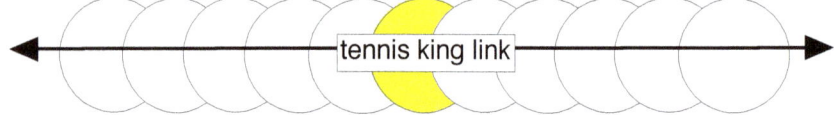

"TENNIS KING EQUATION 2" WRITTEN BY HEAD PRO MARK JOHNS ESPECIALLY FOR YOU.

4

"FOCUS MODELS"

TENNIS KING EQUATION ^{2} "BEYOND THE VORTEX"
OPTIMAL PLAY THROUGH "ENERGY FIELD" RECOGNITION

The Tennis King terminology:

focus models = visual or temporal references that a player focuses on to generate a response

operating system = the programming of the mind to recycle a focus model till play is concluded.

vortex = the location where the gathering energy that creates the response or shot occurs.

vectorization = the creation of vector addresses that guide the shot to a physical destination.

the bridge = a line across the opponent's vortex, used to determine where the shot will go to.

the tunnel = an imaginary reference placed on the opponent's racket before it reaches the vortex bridge.

TENNIS KING EQUATION^2 "BEYOND THE VORTEX"
OPTIMAL PLAY THROUGH "ENERGY FIELD" RECOGNITION

"TENNIS KING EQUATION 2" WRITTEN BY HEAD PRO MARK JOHNS ESPECIALLY FOR YOU.

OPERATING SYSTEMS & FOCUS MODELS

WHY PLAY IN PHYSICAL SPACE IF YOU CAN PLAY IN ADVANCED STATES OF TIME

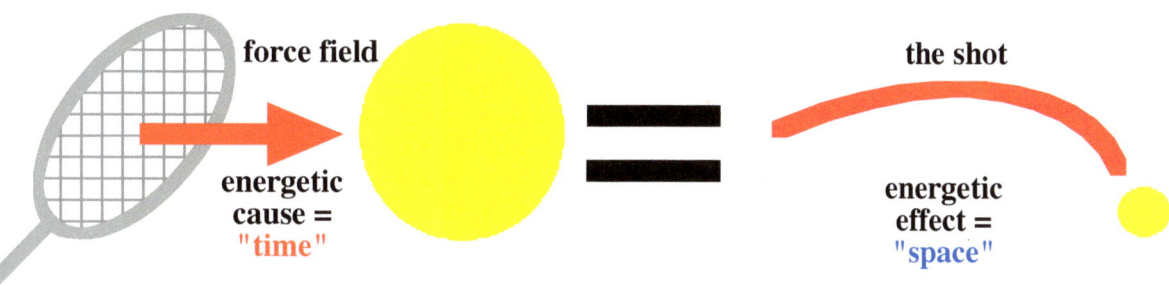

force field — energetic cause = "time"   =   **the shot** — energetic effect = "space"

Every player has their own personal focus model and operating system. Operating systems and focus models are the mental programming that run our tennis game. The focus model is comprised of specific visual focus points in the physical or energetic realms.

Each physical action that we observe has some energetic force field behind it. When a player focuses on the actual physical action, such as a ball being hit with a service motion - our responding return of serve is based on having witnessed the completed serve hitting the ball. Once the serve is seen, then our reaction can begin.

If on the other hand we have a focus model designed to observe the energy patterns that create the serve motion and understand what and where that energy field will send the ball, we can move into our return of serve response before the ball is physically hit. This focus model is a product of "mind over matter" thinking and it will result in "time over space" responses.

The operating system of a player's game is a focus model that captures the total equation of the opponent's shot and the player's reply. A successful operating system recycles with every new shot coming out of the opponent's end of the equation and produces correct responses till the point is over. This recycling process of the focus model is the player's operating system.

Focus models and operating systems can be based on physical space or future times.

⬅ ——— ***tennis king "physics"*** ———➡

Operating systems based in time are superior to physically motivated ones.

TENNIS KING EQUATION ^{2} "BEYOND THE VORTEX"

OPTIMAL PLAY THROUGH "ENERGY FIELD" RECOGNITION

What's in your head? Do you even know how you function during practice and point play. Many players look great in practice and the minute you add a score line to the play - they fall apart. Sound familiar?

The difference between great practice players and great point players is their mental operating systems. The focus model that stands up to tremendous competitive stress is the foundation of the successful operating system.

Great operating systems make great players & great players win matches.

TENNIS KING EQUATION^2 "BEYOND THE VORTEX"
OPTIMAL PLAY THROUGH "ENERGY FIELD" RECOGNITION

"TENNIS KING EQUATION 2" WRITTEN BY HEAD PRO MARK JOHNS ESPECIALLY FOR YOU.

STEP INTO THE VORTEX

AFTER YOU HIT GUARANTEE MAXIMUM VORTEXING POTENTIAL BY PUTTING YOUR BEST FOOT FORWARD

The first step is the most important one. In order to overcome inertia we must energize our response with a step in the right direction. Stepping toward or "into" the opponent's impact vortex initiates the kinetic chain of physical events that represents our next shot in the context of the rally. This is very important because of the timing of this action. We are starting to move even before the opponent has struck the ball.

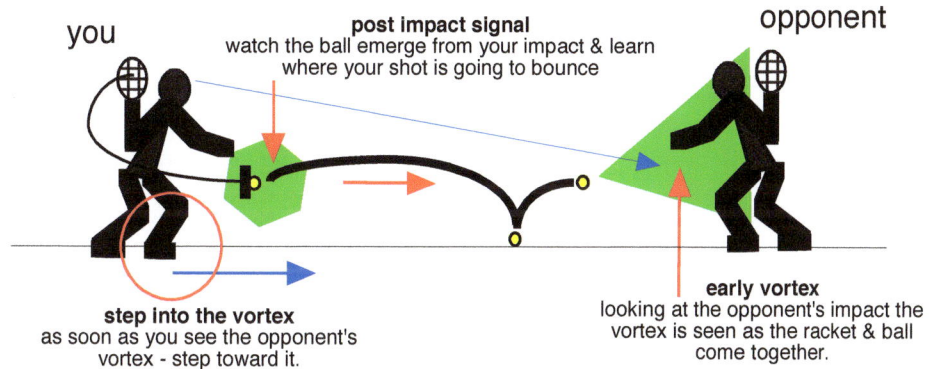

you

post impact signal
watch the ball emerge from your impact & learn where your shot is going to bounce

opponent

step into the vortex
as soon as you see the opponent's vortex - step toward it.

early vortex
looking at the opponent's impact the vortex is seen as the racket & ball come together.

The post impact signal defines where our current shot is going. The signal is received by watching the ball out of our impact. Use this information specifically to move toward "where" our shot is going to bounce. This becomes the origination point of the opponent's vortex and allows us to physically to move toward it with our first step

When you step into the vortex - take your time - you are ahead of schedule.

⬅ *tennis king "physics"* ➡

The player in "time" can move slower then a player in "space"

TENNIS KING EQUATION ² "BEYOND THE VORTEX"
OPTIMAL PLAY THROUGH "ENERGY FIELD" RECOGNITION

Music is the composition of sounds that fit together in a sequential order to create a harmony. When the listener hears a missed note - it is a note that doesn't fit properly into the sequence. This note has a frequency that is dissimilar to the the others. It may be to high or to low, but it is definitely noticeable.

The frequency of any form of energy fluctuates within a prescribed spectrum. This is critical information for the tennis player because it allows a manipulation of calculated energy to create a spectrum of physical responses.

The customization of focus sight-lines means that the player can adjust the frequency of the focus through the mental application of emotion energy compatible to the momentary circumstances.

To hit harder one does not swing harder - the player only needs to focus harder.

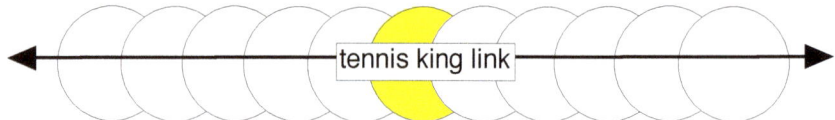

TENNIS KING EQUATION² "BEYOND THE VORTEX"
OPTIMAL PLAY THROUGH "ENERGY FIELD" RECOGNITION

"TENNIS KING EQUATION 2" WRITTEN BY HEAD PRO MARK JOHNS ESPECIALLY FOR YOU.

PAY THE TOLL & GET ON THE BRIDGE

THIS WORKING FOCUS MODEL ALLOWS THE PLAYER TO LOOK INTO THE 3RD DIMENSION OF TIME

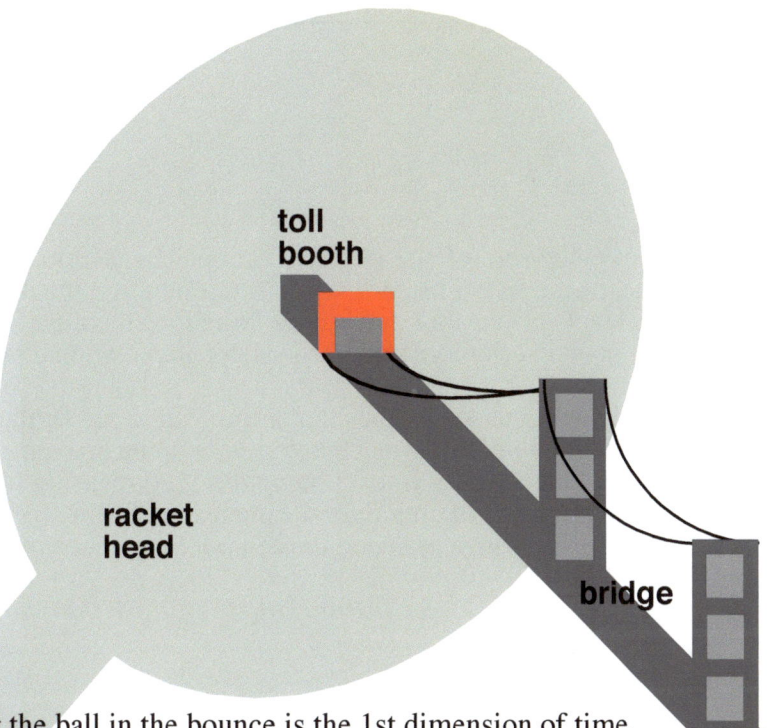

Vectoring the ball in the bounce is the 1st dimension of time. Vortexing the opponent's impact takes you into the 2nd dimension of time. Getting on the bridge and working the toll booth are the 3rd and 4th dimensions of time. What does this mean?

The player who focuses ahead into the progression of action involving the ball is looking into the future. The level of detail seen is the level of information used for the physical response. The "bridge" or vortex axis can be viewed as the racket and ball converge. This level of info can be enhanced by noting the "toll booth" at the start of the bridge. The toll booth is exact moment the opponent's racket comes out of the hacksawing and starts to move toward the ball. When you "work" the toll booth, you know exactly where and when the vector will appear for your addressing and hitting.

Getting on the "bridge" is observing the negative space between the racket and ball.
⬅ ─── ***tennis king "physics"*** ─── ➡
Working the "toll booth" is simply isolating the beginning of the bridge.

TENNIS KING EQUATION ^{2} "BEYOND THE VORTEX"
OPTIMAL PLAY THROUGH "ENERGY FIELD" RECOGNITION

A focus technique is always the start of any physical action. The information you perceive is based on a linear time line. The earlier you see something the more time you have to respond. The levels of play are defined by "when" you collect your information. A professional player sees more info earlier than a recreational player.

The way to improve is to develop focus techniques that allow you to see further and further up the time line. This technique of "bridging" the vortex is in the 3rd dimension of time. The time scale is based on your physical impact being the 1st dimension of space. Then you advance forward to the bounce equaling the 1st dimension of time, followed by the opponent's vortex (#2), the bridge (#3) and the toll booth (#4) of time.

I believe that a super player like Federer sees further into the future than anyone.

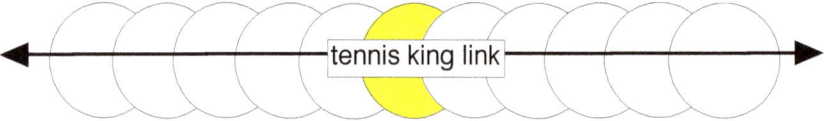

TENNIS KING EQUATION^2 "BEYOND THE VORTEX"
OPTIMAL PLAY THROUGH "ENERGY FIELD" RECOGNITION

"TENNIS KING EQUATION 2" WRITTEN BY HEAD PRO MARK JOHNS ESPECIALLY FOR YOU.

WHAT IS THE PREBRIDGE INDUCTION ?

THE PREBRIDGE INDUCTION PHASE IS THE QUICK WAY TO GET ON THE BRIDGE AND INTO SCALAR

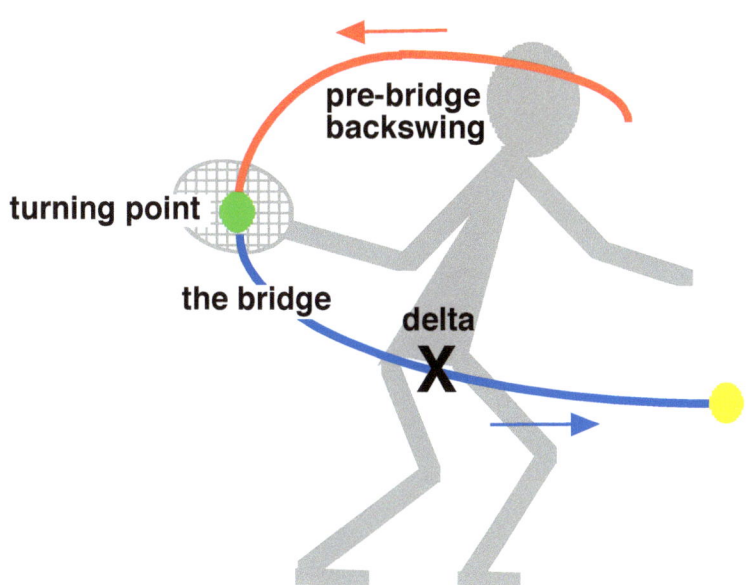

Many players have trouble defining the bridge. A focus sight line on the opponent's racket as it is being brought back will allow you to capture the beginning of "the bridge" just as the racket reaches the "turning point". This is the moment the racket changes direction from back swing to forward swing.

Allow the pre-bridge back swing to physically pull you toward the opponent's impact. This can be considered your induction into the opponent's vortex. During the point keep going back to the opponent's back swing to get pulled onto the bridge. Once your on the bridge and you realize the "delta x" mid span, apply your scalar bar to create your next shot.

Just like priming a pump - the opponent's back swing can pull you in.

⬅——— *tennis king "physics"* ———➡

As you are following your opponent's backswing - maintain an awareness of the ball

TENNIS KING EQUATION ² "BEYOND THE VORTEX"
OPTIMAL PLAY THROUGH "ENERGY FIELD" RECOGNITION

When we watch good players, we see that they are in sync with the give and take action of the point. This allows them to stay in the ball orientation and physically respond simultaneously. This can be accomplished by observing the ball and the opponent's pre-bridge back swing at the same time.

After you start including the opponent's back swing as part of your vortex processing, the bridge awareness occurs quicker. The "turning point" is like a "black hole" of the vortex. This will make more time for placing your "scalar bar" across the bridge.

This induction process will pull you into vortex and your next shot.

TENNIS KING EQUATION ^{2} "BEYOND THE VORTEX"
OPTIMAL PLAY THROUGH "ENERGY FIELD" RECOGNITION

"TENNIS KING EQUATION 2" WRITTEN BY HEAD PRO MARK JOHNS ESPECIALLY FOR YOU.

SCALAR SCOPE THE VORTEX

SCALAR SCOPE WORKS JUST LIKE A SPECTROSCOPE TO DETERMINE ELEMENTAL COMPOSITION

Every vortex is a unique space. Some are long and narrow, while others are short and wide. The vortex axis or bridge is a spectrum of energy running into the ball, creating the physical shot.

The "scalar scope" concept is when the player directs a sight line into the vortex and identifies the "bridge". The isolation of the bridge is the recognition of the energy spectrum, with an awareness of the spectrum increments.

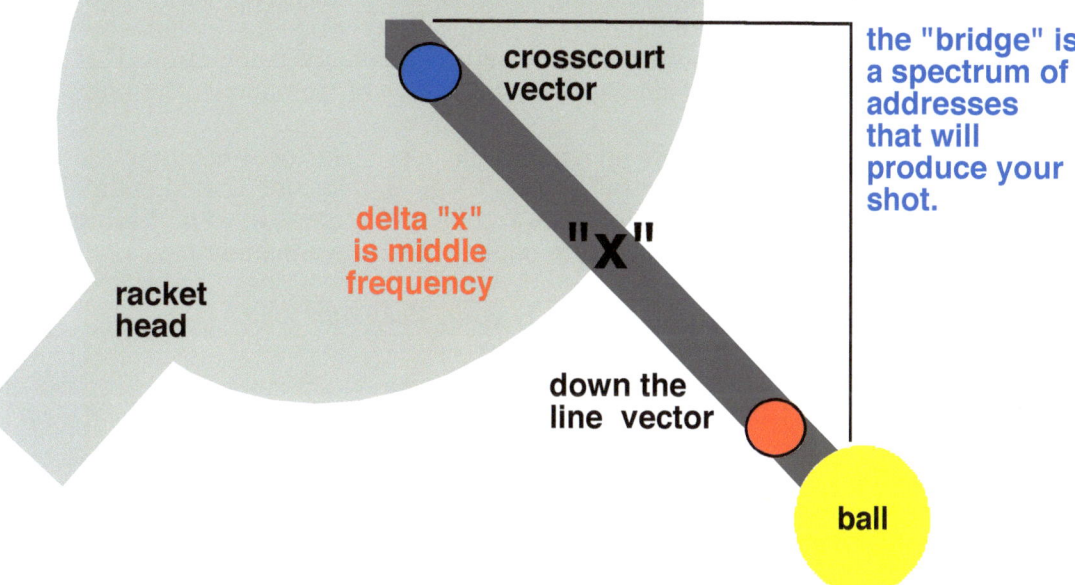

The spectrum is the wavelength of the shot and it can be subdivided by delta "x" a mid frequency point. The player locates delta "x" and from there can now look for a vector address somewhere on the spectrum. A vector found before the mid span will produce a "crosscourt" as your next shot. When a vector located in the 2nd half of the spectrum closer to the ball you are looking at a "down the line" shot as your response.

The wave length and width of the "bridge" is a measure of the shot's energy.

⬅ **tennis king "physics"** ➡

The scalar focus wave is employed by scalar scoping the bridge to locate a vector.

TENNIS KING EQUATION² "BEYOND THE VORTEX"
OPTIMAL PLAY THROUGH "ENERGY FIELD" RECOGNITION

The Tennis King "scalar focus wave" is based on seeing the vector address on the vortex bridge. The focus progression of watching the opponent's vortex (to learn where the ball will bounce) and vector in the bounce (what address do you see on the ball's circumference) are now consolidated into one visual point of recognition. This is the "scalar point" and it is found on the vortex bridge of the opponent's impact.

The "scalar scope" is a focus that increments the vortex axis or "the bridge" into two halves. The first half is the "toll booth" to mid-bridge. All vectors located in the first half are shots that you will hit "crosscourt". The second half vectors, from mid-bridge to the ball are shots that you are going to hit "down the line".

Scalar your opponent by going deep into time !

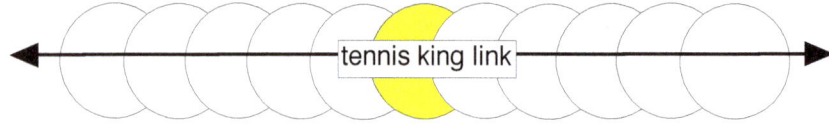

TENNIS KING EQUATION^2 "BEYOND THE VORTEX"
OPTIMAL PLAY THROUGH "ENERGY FIELD" RECOGNITION

"TENNIS KING EQUATION 2" WRITTEN BY HEAD PRO MARK JOHNS ESPECIALLY FOR YOU.

USE A SCALAR BAR TO CREATE THE SHOT

THE SCALAR BAR IS THE IMAGINARY LINE YOU PLACE ACROSS THE VORTEX BRIDGE

opponent impact sample 1

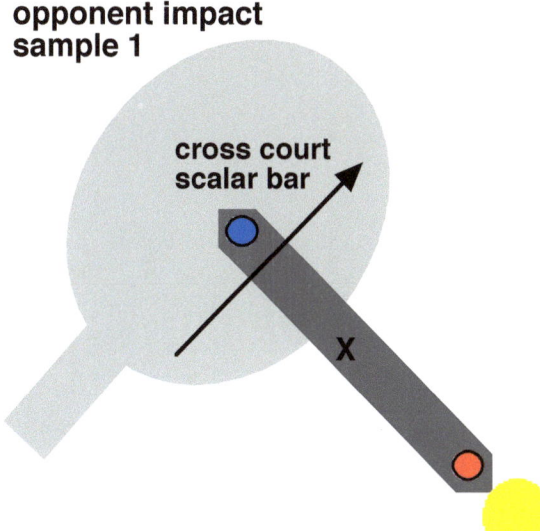

opponent impact sample 2

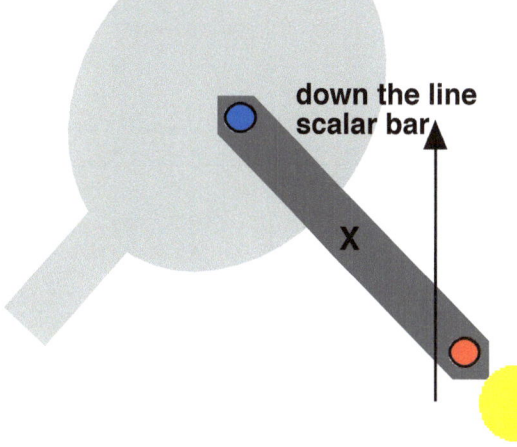

The "scalar bar" is your next focus tool to employee to gain access to an earlier dimension of time. Once you observe the opponent's bridge and determine the delta "X", the "scalar bar" is drawn across the bridge. This line or bar represents the intended swing that will occur in physical space. By holding the "scalar bar" with your conscious mind, the subconscious mind will watch the ball till the moment it can execute the swing that matches the "scalar bar".

The "scalar bar" samples above show a cross court swing and the other a down the line swing. Notice that sample 1 has the "scalar bar" crossing the bridge at the beginning of the bridge and it is positioned directly across the bridge on a right angle. This will produce an earlier physical swing than sample 2. The down the line "scalar bar" has the swing crossing the bridge later and intersecting with an angle parallel with the court's side line.

The scalar bar allows you to metally hit your shot before the opponent has hit the ball.

←——— tennis king "physics" ———→

Incrementing of the vortex bridge creates an understanding of which shots are possible.

TENNIS KING EQUATION ^{2} "BEYOND THE VORTEX"
OPTIMAL PLAY THROUGH "ENERGY FIELD" RECOGNITION

The "scalar bar" is like a visual crow bar in the task of gaining earlier dimensions of time. The "scalar bar" is drawn across the vortex bridge to create the swing that will result when the player holds the "scalar bar" in the conscious mind for the duration of the physical unfolding of the event. The way a player views the bridge also indicates what shots are physically feasible by the way the scalar bar fits into the picture.

When the vortex bridge presents itself it will show you which exposures are approachable and which are not. Trying to force a shot not available in the bridge perspective will always result in an error. Seeing the bridge is your crystal ball into the immediate future.

You gain tremendous physical leverage when you apply the scalar bar.

TENNIS KING EQUATION^2 "BEYOND THE VORTEX"
OPTIMAL PLAY THROUGH "ENERGY FIELD" RECOGNITION

"TENNIS KING EQUATION 2" WRITTEN BY HEAD PRO MARK JOHNS ESPECIALLY FOR YOU.

MICRO AND MACRO MANAGEMENT

SCALAR BAR SIZING IS BASED ON THE TYPE VORTEX BRIDGE AND THE SHOT YOU HIT.

micro scalar bars   **macro scalar bars**

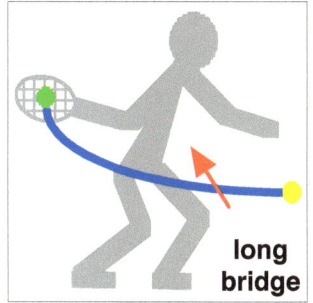
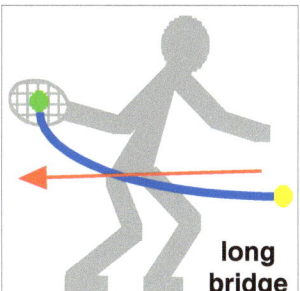

The same bridge can be approached with different scalar bars. This long bridge can be "micro barred" to hit a short angle or "macro barred" to hit a deep baseline shot.

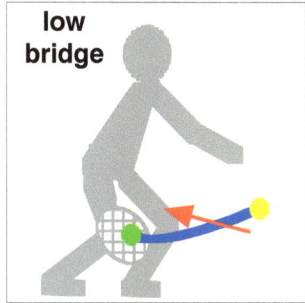
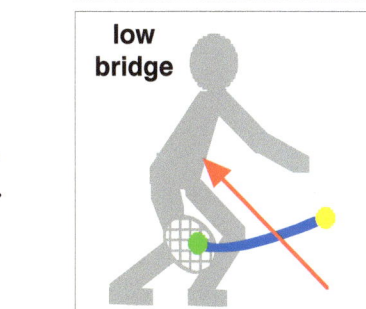

This low bridge is "micro barred" to hit a short ball or "macro barred" to hit a deep heavy topspin approach shot.

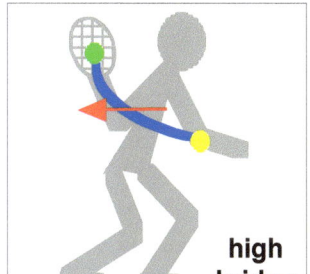
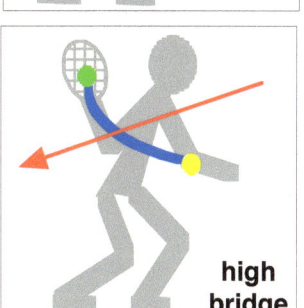

A high bridge can be "micro barred" to hit a flat passing shot or "macro barred" to create a deep heavy slice shot.

The "micro bar" is intended to create shots that use consistency and placement to displace the opponent. The "macro bar" is used to overpower or push the opponent around. Personal style dictates what your "micro/macro" bar code is in your game. Players need to be aware that certain bridges require specific scalar bars.

The micro bar generates an efficient and consistent use of energy.

⬅ ─── *tennis king "physics"* ─── ➡

The macro bar uses more energy and it is not as reliable - so it should be less employed.

TENNIS KING EQUATION ^{2} "BEYOND THE VORTEX"
OPTIMAL PLAY THROUGH "ENERGY FIELD" RECOGNITION

Many players try to push the envelop to the max by using power to excess. This leads to a game loaded with unforced errors. The macro approach of always hitting big shots to overwhelm the opponent is really just a reflection of a fearful emotional state of mind. The player wants to get out of the point as quickly as possible and at any cost..

..even if it means losing the point.

To be truly competitive a player needs to balance the risk ratio to a realistic and productive level. This means allowing the opponent's vortex bridge a chance to provide you with both macro and micro options. The micro approach allows you to play within the court and this eliminates the unforced errors. Playing a "small" or using a micro game plan means that you can dictate the play without risking the point.

The scalar "micro bar" is a safe way to setting up the point without risking the point.

TENNIS KING EQUATION ^{2} "BEYOND THE VORTEX"
OPTIMAL PLAY THROUGH "ENERGY FIELD" RECOGNITION

"TENNIS KING EQUATION 2" WRITTEN BY HEAD PRO MARK JOHNS ESPECIALLY FOR YOU.

MICRO AND MACRO BAR CODES

SCALAR BAR SIMPLIFIED TO A LINE DRAWING RECOGNITION CREATES QUICKER RESPONSES

bridges and bars

bar code diagrams

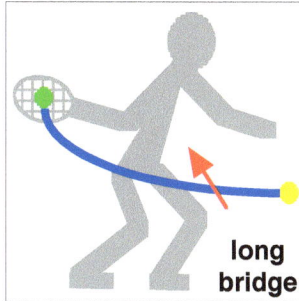

long bridge

The bridge and bar diagram on the left can be mentally reduced to the line diagram on the right. Note micro bars are arrows starting "on the bridge" and macro bars go "through the bridge".

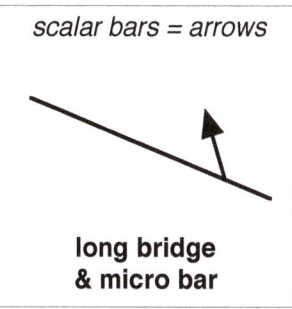

scalar bars = arrows

long bridge & micro bar

low bridge

This simple 2 line configuration represents your opponent's shot and your shot before either is transacted into physical space.

low bridge & macro bar

high bridge

A pattern of bridges and bars will become apparent during the course of the match. You can adjust your bar response to influence bridge patterns.

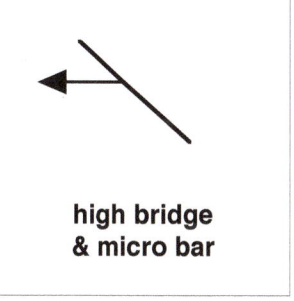

high bridge & micro bar

The the reduction of vortex bridges and scalar bars from event level recognitions to a simple 2 line diagram accelerates the understanding of the "cause and effect" patterns of point play. The earlier you see it - the earlier you hit it. This is how you put the pressure on your opponent.

What "comes around - goes around" is true in tennis.

← *tennis king "physics"* →

The scalar bar you place on the bridge will become the bridge in your impact.

TENNIS KING EQUATION ² "BEYOND THE VORTEX"

OPTIMAL PLAY THROUGH "ENERGY FIELD" RECOGNITION

The use of symbols in our lives is universal. They inform and direct us simultaneously. The concept that the entire evaluation and response system can be symbolized by 2 lines is a conscious mental process that reduces the time factor in your favor.

The best players realize patterns instinctively and respond immediately. This is why they are the best players. The mind is not meant to be weighted down by a "thought process". The bridge and bar diagram is a visual recognition that represents two physical actions. They are your opponent's shot and your shot, both seen before they occur.

If you thinking during the point - you are losing the point.

TENNIS KING EQUATION ^{2} "BEYOND THE VORTEX"
OPTIMAL PLAY THROUGH "ENERGY FIELD" RECOGNITION

"TENNIS KING EQUATION 2" WRITTEN BY HEAD PRO MARK JOHNS ESPECIALLY FOR YOU.

THE VECTORIZATION OF THE VORTEX

ONCE YOU PUT THE VORTEX BRIDGE INSIDE A BUBBLE - YOUR VECTOR ADDRESS IS ON THE BRIDGE.

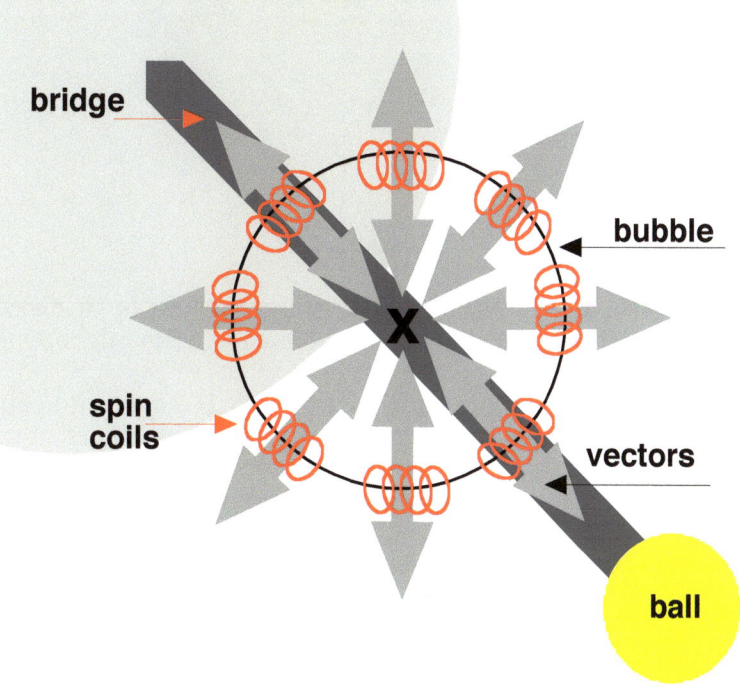

The bridge can be manipulated. The focus can find details on the vortex bridge that can be used to create an infinite number of shots compatible to any situation. This focus technique works off the "delta x". The player takes the "x" and bubbles it. This bubble can enclose the entire bridge or just the "x".

Once the bubble is in your consciousness, use it as a vector address. You do this by taking your "scalar bar" and intersecting the bubble on angles to equal your intended physical shot. Manipulating the bubble with a scalar bar can also include hitting different spins and velocities This is done by running the scalar bar across the bubble the same way you would manipulate a tennis ball with your racket. Topspin is a upward moving bar and slice is a downward bar movement. Hitting the ball harder or softer is a measure of scalar bar intensity.

Manipulating the bubble is the exact precursor of your physical shot.
←——— tennis king "physics" ———→
The advantage of "bubble bridging" is that it advances your physical response in time.

TENNIS KING EQUATION² "BEYOND THE VORTEX"
OPTIMAL PLAY THROUGH "ENERGY FIELD" RECOGNITION

This mental construction of "vectoring the bridge" results in physical step forward into a future time dimension. You actually start your swing before the opponent has hit the ball.

This is how the player can employ a "time over space" concept to gain an advantage over the opponent. Another by product of this focus technique is that there is "no ball". The player is preoccupied with bubbling and vectoring the bridge that the conscious awareness of the ball disappears until after you hit the ball.

When you "bubble the bridge" there is "no ball!".

TENNIS KING EQUATION ^{2} "BEYOND THE VORTEX"
OPTIMAL PLAY THROUGH "ENERGY FIELD" RECOGNITION

"TENNIS KING EQUATION 2" WRITTEN BY HEAD PRO MARK JOHNS ESPECIALLY FOR YOU.

THE "GOLDEN TRIANGLE" THEORY

A VECTOR SATELLITE ADDRESS OFF THE VORTEX BRIDGE CAN VEX YOUR OPPONENT

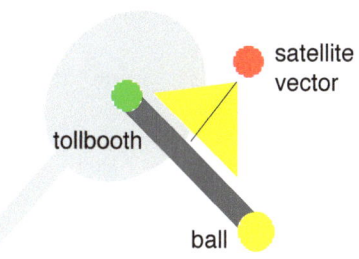

The satellite vector address is to be found at the end of the scalar bar. This bridge and bar diagram shows a micro bar originating mid bridge and extending to the red vector address.

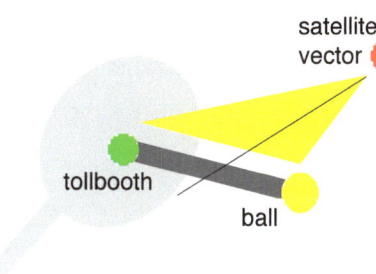

How to manipulate a satellite address is easy. Start by creating the bridge and then run the scalar bar toward a point of destination. At the terminate point of the bar is your satellite address.

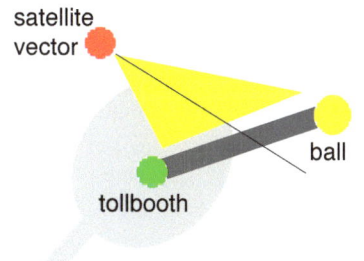

Once the satellite vector address is up and running, you have your triangle. Drop the bar and the bridge. Just hold the satellite vector address till after the ball comes out of your impact.

The "golden triangle" is the resultant of the bridge ends and your destination point.

⬅ *tennis king "physics"* ➡

The type of vortex bridge will dictate the type of triangle you can create.

TENNIS KING EQUATION² "BEYOND THE VORTEX"
OPTIMAL PLAY THROUGH "ENERGY FIELD" RECOGNITION

The "golden triangle" means your shot is golden. Once you have the two bridge coordinates they will automatically create the "vector sum".

This vector sum will equal a satellite address located off the bridge that in line with your intended shot destination. The three points create the "golden triangle". This polygon insures that your shot is founded on solid physics principles and will not fail.

Once you have the triangle your are golden!

TENNIS KING EQUATION^2 "BEYOND THE VORTEX"
OPTIMAL PLAY THROUGH "ENERGY FIELD" RECOGNITION

"TENNIS KING EQUATION 2" WRITTEN BY HEAD PRO MARK JOHNS ESPECIALLY FOR YOU.

"RING FOR SERVICE" TO HOLD YOUR SERVE

CREATE A "RING" ON THE SERVE TOSS TO FUNNEL YOUR ENERGY INTO THE SERVICE BOX

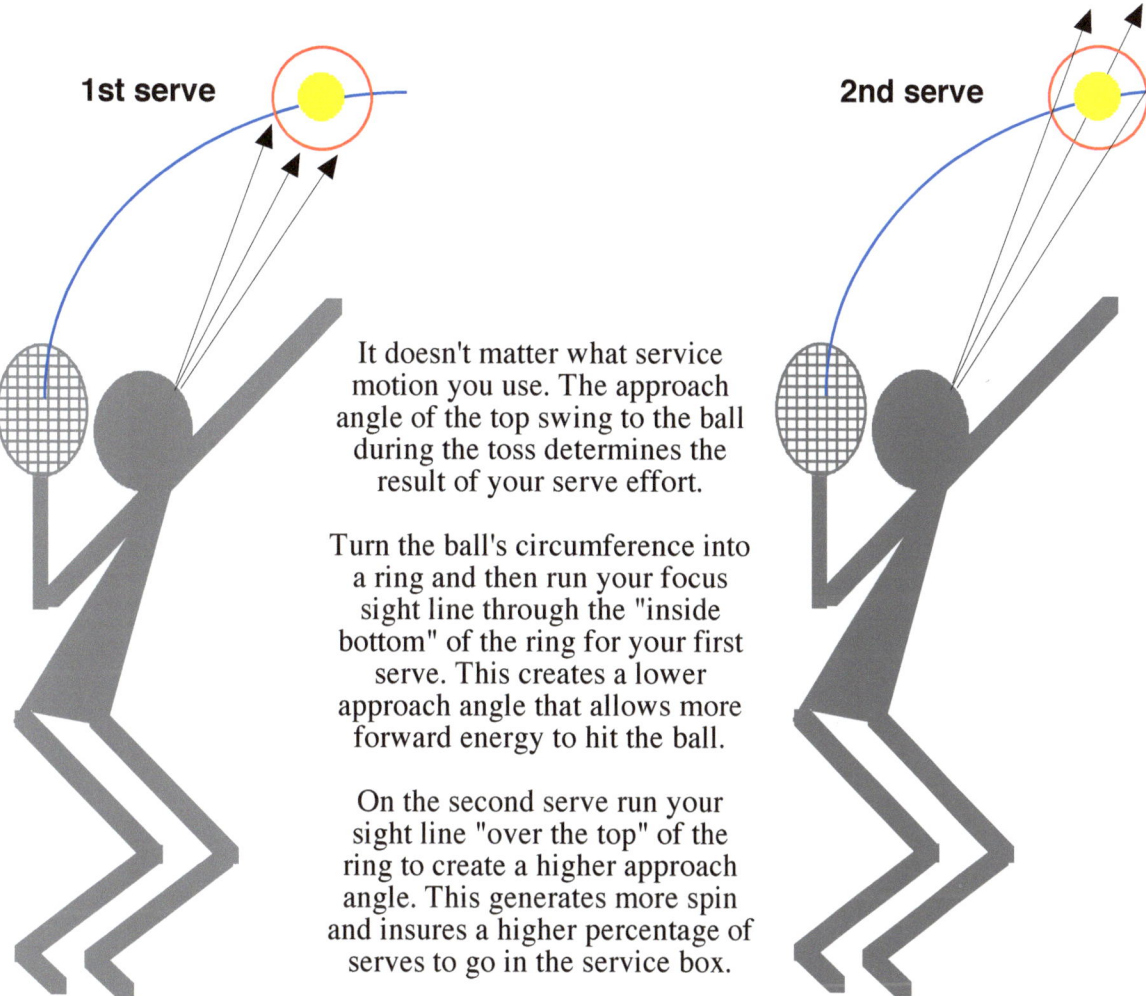

It doesn't matter what service motion you use. The approach angle of the top swing to the ball during the toss determines the result of your serve effort.

Turn the ball's circumference into a ring and then run your focus sight line through the "inside bottom" of the ring for your first serve. This creates a lower approach angle that allows more forward energy to hit the ball.

On the second serve run your sight line "over the top" of the ring to create a higher approach angle. This generates more spin and insures a higher percentage of serves to go in the service box.

The reduction of the serve to a sight line running through a ring is simple as it gets.

⟵ tennis king "physics" ⟶

The first and second serve both maintain racketed speed - only directed differently.

TENNIS KING EQUATION² "BEYOND THE VORTEX"
OPTIMAL PLAY THROUGH "ENERGY FIELD" RECOGNITION

The serve is the foundation of most player's games. The ability to hold serve is critical to winning. The stress level encountered during serving should be reduced to a manageable level. Reducing the serve to a mental construction of a ring with addresses can do this.

The ring is the ball's circumference without the physical ball to distract the server. The lower ring addresses will produce a more horizontal angle for the swing into the ball. This is going to generate a more powerful serve, while the top ring addresses will cause a more vertical swing and more spin on the ball. The spin and vertical approach are perfect for second serving because of the high probability of the ball going into the service box.

By simplifying the focus to the service "ring" will create a better serve game.

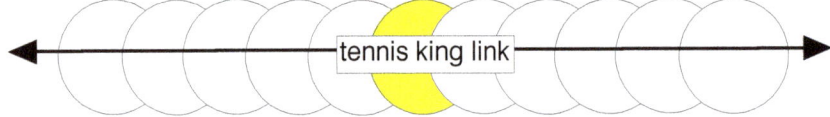

TENNIS KING EQUATION^2 "BEYOND THE VORTEX"
OPTIMAL PLAY THROUGH "ENERGY FIELD" RECOGNITION

"TENNIS KING EQUATION 2" WRITTEN BY HEAD PRO MARK JOHNS ESPECIALLY FOR YOU.

VIRTUAL VECTOR "C" VISION

ON THE TOSS SEE THE REFLECTION OF THE EXACT SPOT ON THE COURT WHERE VECTOR "C" WILL BE

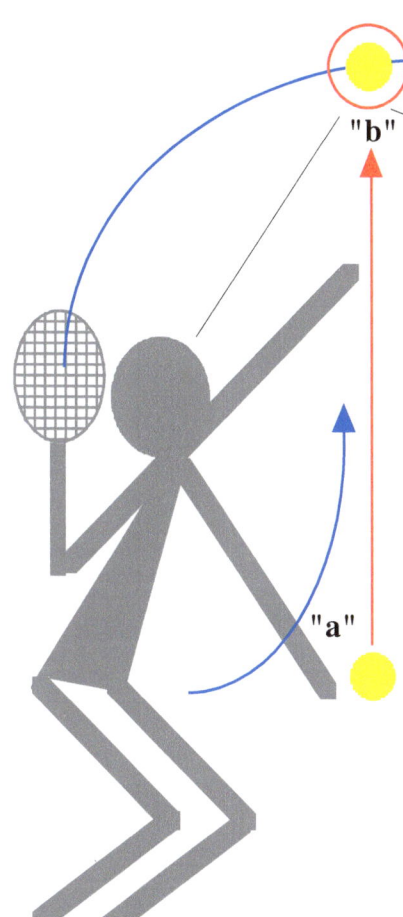

The sequence of the service motion and the moment you address the toss is the basis of your timing on the serve.

A. When the toss hand and the racket reach the bottom of their motion - address in your mind the ball as you imagine it will look like at the top of the toss.

B. When the sight-line runs up to the address on the ball toss - visualize the vector "c" in the service box and swing completely through the "b" holding the vector "c" in your head till the ball comes off your racket.

C. Once the ball has left your racket - place your sight-line into the bounce of the serve (vector "c") and pick up the bridge or the tunnel to address your next shot.

This focus model is to overcome a tendency to hit up to ball and not thru the ball.

⟵ ——— *tennis king "physics"* ——— ⟶

Turning the toss into a reflective device to see vector "c" - you will hit thru the ball.

TENNIS KING EQUATION² "BEYOND THE VORTEX"
OPTIMAL PLAY THROUGH "ENERGY FIELD" RECOGNITION

The momentum of the swing at the ball's impact is dependent largely where you imagine the end of your swing will be. Many players lose control of the serve because they hit up to the toss and then the swing fades quickly.

The virtual "c" on the bottom of the ball at the address you want to hit helps you to realize that the swing is not complete till it generates enough power to send the ball to the service box location that you want to hit.

The reflection of the actual court on the toss will empower your swing to completion.

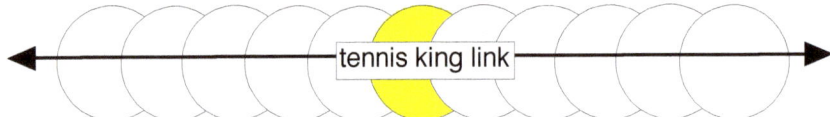

TENNIS KING EQUATION ^{2} "BEYOND THE VORTEX"
OPTIMAL PLAY THROUGH "ENERGY FIELD" RECOGNITION

"TENNIS KING EQUATION 2" WRITTEN BY HEAD PRO MARK JOHNS ESPECIALLY FOR YOU.

ASTRAL PROJECTION IS AS SIMPLE AS "A-B-C"

THIS IS YOUR GOLDEN TRIANGLE POWERED BY THE SUPER NATURAL

astral body = a supersensible substance pervading space and forming the substance of a second body belonging to each individual.

astral projection = the act of separating the astral body (the consciousness) from the physical body and it's journey into the universe

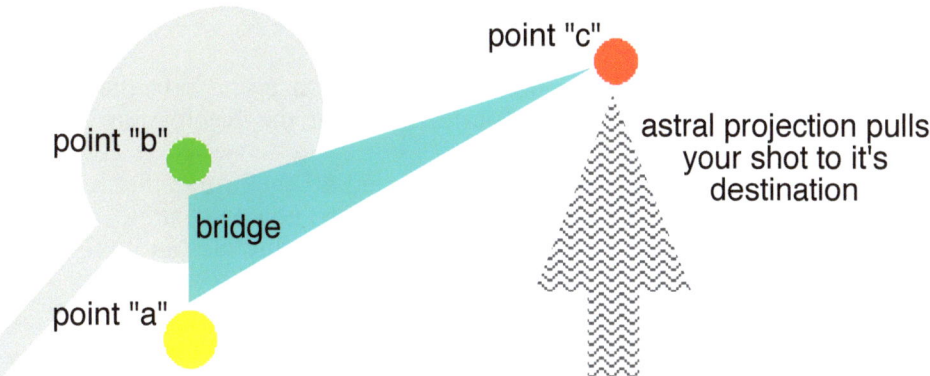

The astral body can move out of our physical body. Consider the astral body your spirit or consciousness. This allows us an "out of body experience" where we can look down on our own body from a higher or removed vantage point. This is out of body function is done through astral projection.

The focus technique "the golden triangle" is formed by the bridge and your shot destination. This triangle is defined as "a" the ball - "b" the racket - "c" the destination for your shot. During the memorization of the "a-b" bridge the player realizes point "c". Rather than trying to hit point "c" allow it to pull you and your swing toward it. Point "c" possesses a very power attraction that creates an astral projection that moves our consciousness to this point on the court. The swing and the resulting shot will automatically go to point "c" by way of a subconscious compliance to the astral projection.

Moving your consciousness out of your body creates a tremendous advantage

← *tennis king "physics"* →

Once you are free of the body's physical restrictions - shot making becomes easy.

TENNIS KING EQUATION ^{2} "BEYOND THE VORTEX"
OPTIMAL PLAY THROUGH "ENERGY FIELD" RECOGNITION

The "golden triangle" means your shot is golden. Once you have the two bridge coordinates they will automatically create the "vector sum".

This vector sum will equal a satellite address located off the bridge that in line with your intended shot destination. The three points create the "golden triangle". This polygon insures that your shot is founded on solid physics principles and will not fail.

Once you have the triangle your are golden!

TENNIS KING EQUATION ^{2} "BEYOND THE VORTEX"
OPTIMAL PLAY THROUGH "ENERGY FIELD" RECOGNITION

"TENNIS KING EQUATION 2" WRITTEN BY HEAD PRO MARK JOHNS ESPECIALLY FOR YOU.

TO "B" OR NOT TO "B" - THAT IS THE QUESTION

THE VERTICES "B" OF THE GOLDEN TRIANGLE IS THE PIVOT POINT OF YOUR PHYSICAL RESPONSE

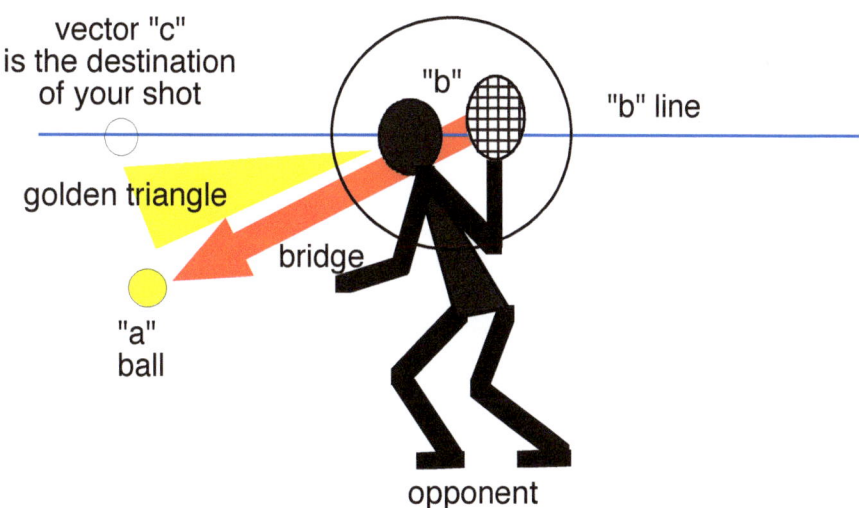

The vertices "b" is the turning point of your opponent's swing. This is the moment the swing turns on to the final approach of the ball. To "b" or not to "b" is critical to your subconscious calculations on the entire physical reply of your shot. When you view vertices "b" all the variables of time and space are realized and accounted for. This is the exact information required to hit from your subconscious.

Your focus sight line after you hit the ball is directed onto the opponent's racket during it;s hacksawing and when it turns back towards the ball you memorize this point in time. It represents vertices "b" of the golden triangle. Once this is noted your focus will automatically produce the vector "c", the intended destination of your next shot.

Once you hit your shot zoom your focus sight line into your opponent's back swing.

⬅ *tennis king "physics"* ➡

When focusing on opponent's serve - use the upward motion of the toss as vertices "b".

TENNIS KING EQUATION ^{2} "BEYOND THE VORTEX"
OPTIMAL PLAY THROUGH "ENERGY FIELD" RECOGNITION

The moment of truth is in the vertices "b" of your opponent's golden triangle. This split second recognition is the only way to guarantee you will not choke on your next reply. That's right all choking originates from having not observed this most important "turning point" in time.

The recognition of the "b" point is extremely easy - you just look for it and when it appears you will know it.

To "b" or not not to "b" is the difference between success and failure.

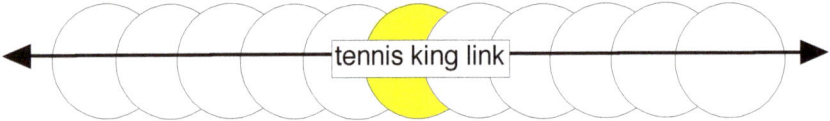

TENNIS KING EQUATION ^{2} "BEYOND THE VORTEX"
OPTIMAL PLAY THROUGH "ENERGY FIELD" RECOGNITION

"TENNIS KING EQUATION 2" WRITTEN BY HEAD PRO MARK JOHNS ESPECIALLY FOR YOU.

WANT TO GET THERE FAST - TAKE THE "B" LINE

FIND YOUR VECTOR "C" ON THE "B" LINE AND YOU WILL BLOW AWAY THE COMPETITION

Your opponent's a big hitter and your are feeling overwhelmed by his power. This is not a problem if you "take the "b" line" to vector "c". The "b" line is quick and easy to use. It is a horizontal line that runs through the vertices "b" to create an event horizon for your next shot.

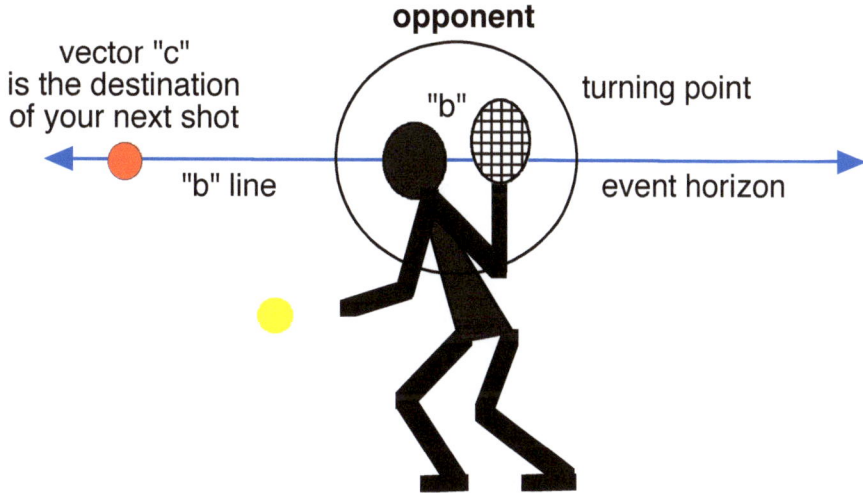

As the opponent's racket starts forward mark "b" and run the horizontal line through it from one side of the court to the other. During this millisecond process vector "c" will show up on the event horizon. Memorize and hold "c" till your shot is completed and you will have hit to your intended placement.

The management of vertices "b" is always critical to hitting your next shot.

←——— tennis king "physics" ———→

The "b line" is a quick way to get ahead of the big hitters without self destructing.

TENNIS KING EQUATION² "BEYOND THE VORTEX"
OPTIMAL PLAY THROUGH "ENERGY FIELD" RECOGNITION

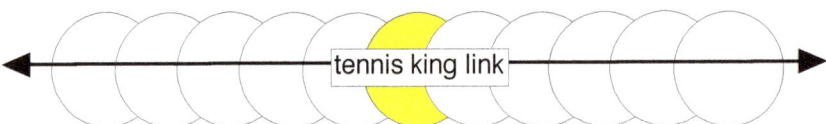

The Tennis King Equation² is a number of focus models designed to generate quality physical play effortlessly by staying ahead of physical space.

The "b line" is a focus model that is meant to quicken our response to neutralize the loss of time produced by hard hitting opponents. All of the Tennis King focus models are based on the "time over space" concept to minimize physical effort in our play.

A player without a "focus model" is a player in big trouble.

TENNIS KING EQUATION² "BEYOND THE VORTEX"
OPTIMAL PLAY THROUGH "ENERGY FIELD" RECOGNITION

"TENNIS KING EQUATION 2" WRITTEN BY HEAD PRO MARK JOHNS ESPECIALLY FOR YOU.

THE DOUBLE "D" WORKS FINE FOR ME

THIS IS A FOCUS MODEL IS WHERE TWO DOTS ARE ALL YOU NEED TO HIT YOUR SHOT.

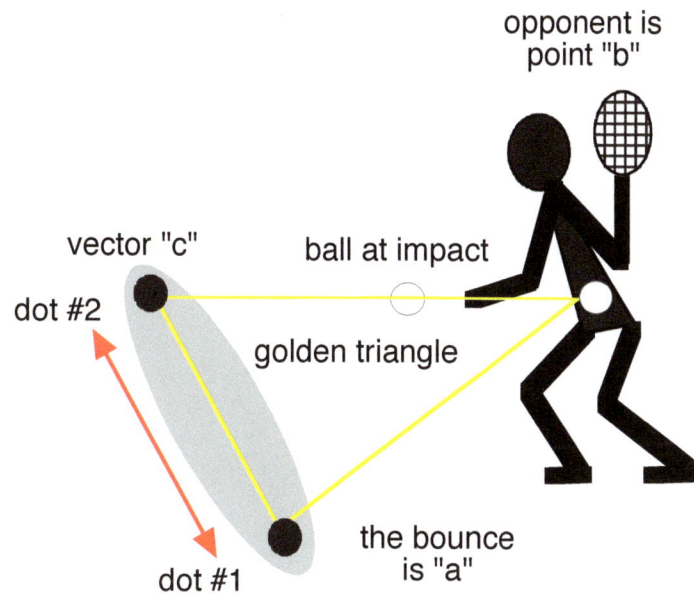

The double dot focus model above is a very quick and super easy way to bridge the opponent's impact while establishing your shot's destination.

The first step is to note the bounce location as dot #1 and then relate that dot to your opponent's body. This will establish the vortex or "a-b" bridge, revealing to your subconscious the direction of your opponent's shot.

The second dot is conjured consciously somewhere off the "a-b" bridge to form the golden triangle. Hold dot #2 as your vector "c" till your shot is complete and the ball is out of your racket. This process of double dotting that's only .25 seconds.

The double "d" focus model is a very simple and quick way to create your shot.
←——— tennis king "physics" ———→
The creation of the golden triangle insures physical and strategical stability.

TENNIS KING EQUATION² "BEYOND THE VORTEX"
OPTIMAL PLAY THROUGH "ENERGY FIELD" RECOGNITION

The double "d" model is a mental construction of vector "c" after you have defined the bounce and the opponent's position. The generation of your shot to vector "c" is completion of this model. The model is recycled as long as needed to win the point and constitutes your operating system of your game.

The double "d" works on the return of serve by noting the ball's release on the opponent's toss as dot #1 and the turning point of the service motion as point "b". The 2nd dot is established somewhere on the court by the consciousness and held as vector "c".

The basis of any operating system requires a strong focus model.

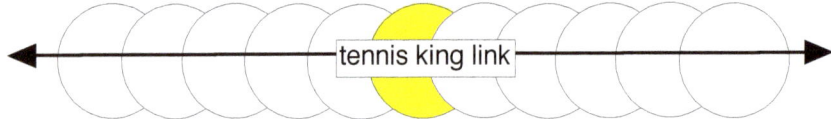

TENNIS KING EQUATION^2 "BEYOND THE VORTEX"
OPTIMAL PLAY THROUGH "ENERGY FIELD" RECOGNITION

"TENNIS KING EQUATION 2" WRITTEN BY HEAD PRO MARK JOHNS ESPECIALLY FOR YOU.

NO TWO BALL PRINTS ARE ALIKE

THE SHOT YOU JUST HIT IS ABOUT TO BOUNCE - PREPARE TO MEMORIZE IT'S BALL PRINT

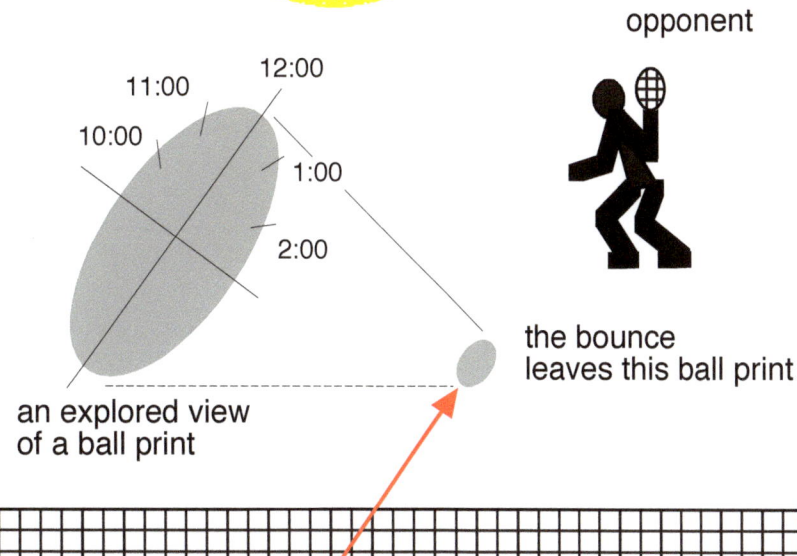

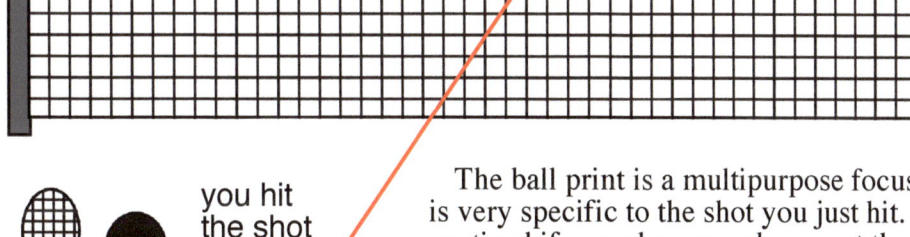

you hit the shot

The ball print is a multipurpose focus tool. It is very specific to the shot you just hit. You have noticed if you play on a clay court that shots of different velocities and spins leave unique ball prints. The realization of a ball print in your conscious mind after hitting the serve or shot allows you time to memorize this print and convert it into a focus reference to generate your next shot. Hold the ball print till you see clock increments along it's outline. Use these time addresses to create your vector "c'. The holding on to the memory of the print with a time address not only permits you to direct your shot, it also occupies your conscious mind during the hitting process.

The ball print reads your opponent's impact and permits you to hit your next shot.

⟵ tennis king "physics" ⟶

This intergration of function produce extra time to physically respond.

TENNIS KING EQUATION² "BEYOND THE VORTEX"

OPTIMAL PLAY THROUGH "ENERGY FIELD" RECOGNITION

The "ball print" works in several dimensions of time, allowing you the benefit of having more time to hit confidentially. The first dimension of time is the recognition of the actual ball print after hitting your shot. You hit and in your conscious mind produce a realization of what type of print your shot is going to leave once it hits the court.

The second dimension of time is the clock like increments surrounding the print's outline. They create the address to your next shot's destination or vector "c". Holding this image of the memorized ball print with the vector "c" address generates your next shot before your opponent has even hit his shot. The 3rd dimension of time occurs during the holding of the ball print memory while your subconscious mind records the opponent's swing and deduces it's destination. This initiates your footwork to position for your next shot.

The ball print gives you three dimensions of time at the cost on one.

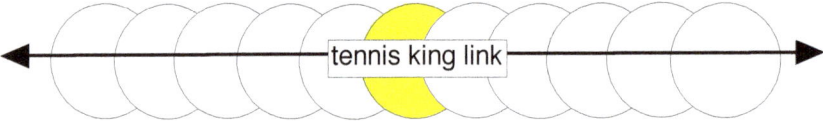

TENNIS KING EQUATION ^{2} "BEYOND THE VORTEX"
OPTIMAL PLAY THROUGH "ENERGY FIELD" RECOGNITION

"TENNIS KING EQUATION 2" WRITTEN BY HEAD PRO MARK JOHNS ESPECIALLY FOR YOU.

THE "GREAT TRIANGLE" FOR A SURE SHOT

THE SIMPLE A-B-C TRIANGLE IS THE QUICKEST AND EASIEST FOCUS MODEL OF ALL!

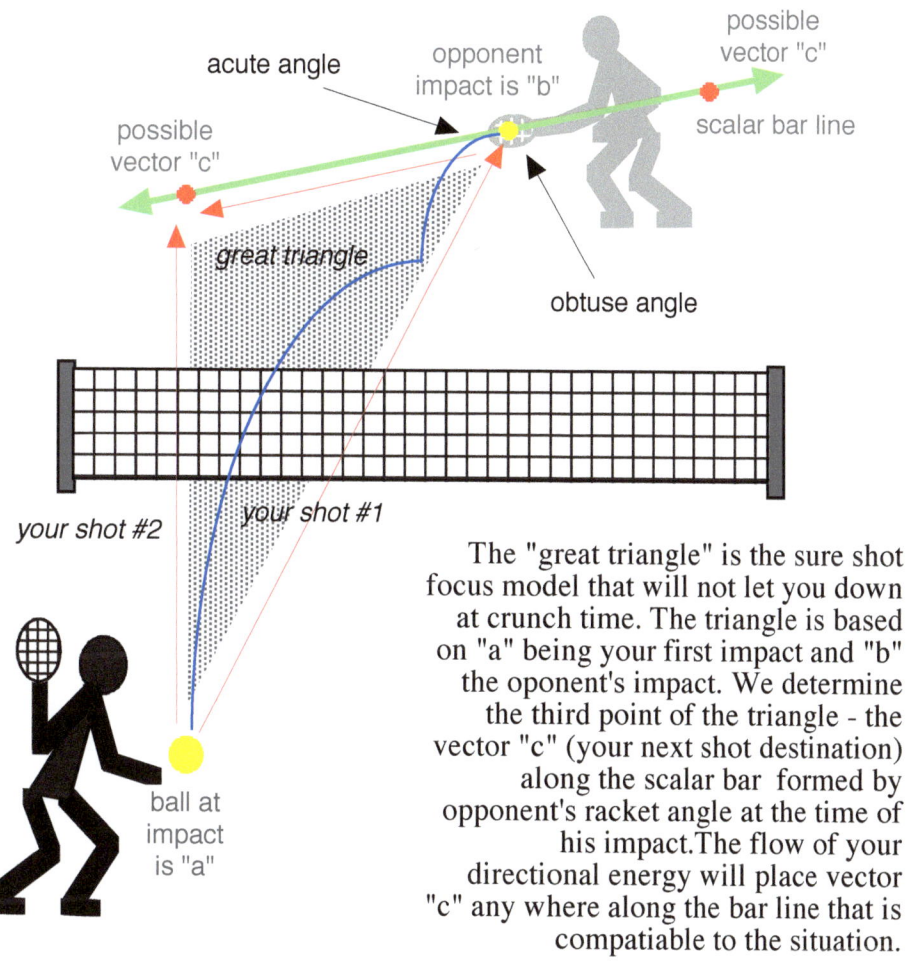

The "great triangle" is the sure shot focus model that will not let you down at crunch time. The triangle is based on "a" being your first impact and "b" the opponent's impact. We determine the third point of the triangle - the vector "c" (your next shot destination) along the scalar bar formed by opponent's racket angle at the time of his impact. The flow of your directional energy will place vector "c" any where along the bar line that is compatible to the situation.

The "great triangle" hinges on the opponent's racket angle during his impact.

←——— tennis king "physics" ———→

The extension of the racket angle in either direction will work as the base of the triangle.

TENNIS KING EQUATION² "BEYOND THE VORTEX"
OPTIMAL PLAY THROUGH "ENERGY FIELD" RECOGNITION

The relationship of the ball and the opponent's racket at the moment of impact is the vertex "b" of the "great triangle". This corner of the triangle is formed by two lines. The first line is the trajectory line of your shot from the bounce to the opponent's impact and the second is by the angle of the racket during the impact.

Seeing this angular corner as either acute or obtuse will generate your next shot's destination - this third point of the great triangle is your vector "c".

Once again point "b" allows you to "corner" the market for your vector "c".

TENNIS KING EQUATION² "BEYOND THE VORTEX"
OPTIMAL PLAY THROUGH "ENERGY FIELD" RECOGNITION

"TENNIS KING EQUATION 2" WRITTEN BY HEAD PRO MARK JOHNS ESPECIALLY FOR YOU.

THE ANGULAR COMPRESSION & DILATION OF TIME

USING ACUTE AND OBTUSE TRIANGLES TO COMPRESS OR DILATE THE TIME FRAME

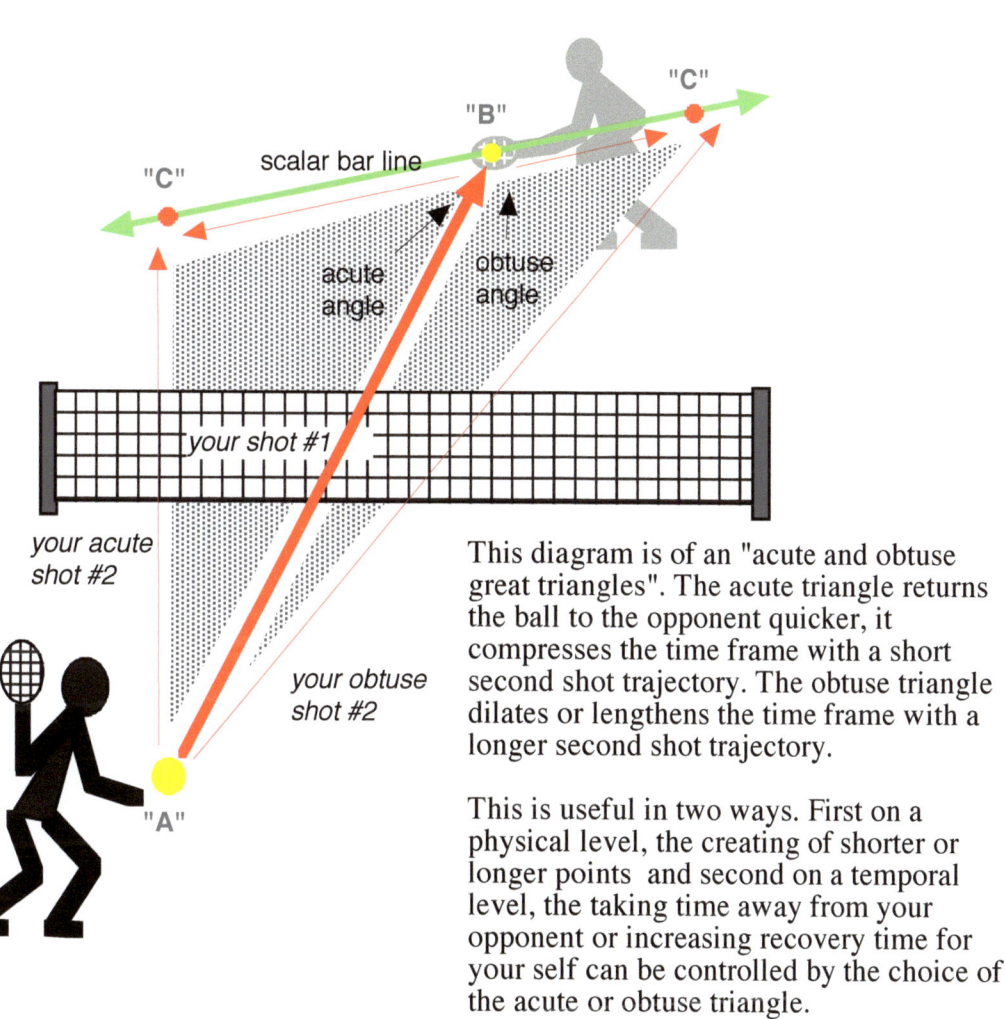

This diagram is of an "acute and obtuse great triangles". The acute triangle returns the ball to the opponent quicker, it compresses the time frame with a short second shot trajectory. The obtuse triangle dilates or lengthens the time frame with a longer second shot trajectory.

This is useful in two ways. First on a physical level, the creating of shorter or longer points and second on a temporal level, the taking time away from your opponent or increasing recovery time for your self can be controlled by the choice of the acute or obtuse triangle.

Once again the manipulation of time allows us to control the physical realm.

The selection of the acute or obtuse triangle is determined by your position in time.

TENNIS KING EQUATION^2 "BEYOND THE VORTEX"
OPTIMAL PLAY THROUGH "ENERGY FIELD" RECOGNITION

The process of shot selection is largely an automatic function of the unconscious. There are adjustments that the conscious mind install during non-play moments. The idea of strategy comes to mind in this instance. The player can preprogram the subconscious to a particular strategy and revise it at any time. Once a strategy is programed the player automatically seeks out opportunities to implement the plan.

This is where the dilation and compression of time enters the picture. A net rushing strategy would use compression of the time frame (acute angle off the bridge) to press the opponent and a long rally strategy would use the dilation of time (obtuse angle) to extend the length of the point.

When you manipulate time - you control the play.

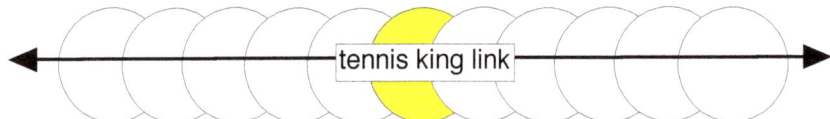

TENNIS KING EQUATION^2 "BEYOND THE VORTEX"
OPTIMAL PLAY THROUGH "ENERGY FIELD" RECOGNITION

"TENNIS KING EQUATION 2" WRITTEN BY HEAD PRO MARK JOHNS ESPECIALLY FOR YOU.

TAKE THE TUNNEL - IT'S FASTER THAN THE BRIDGE

THE PRE-BRIDGE TUNNEL IS FASTER WHEN YOU ARE LOOKING FOR VECTOR "C"

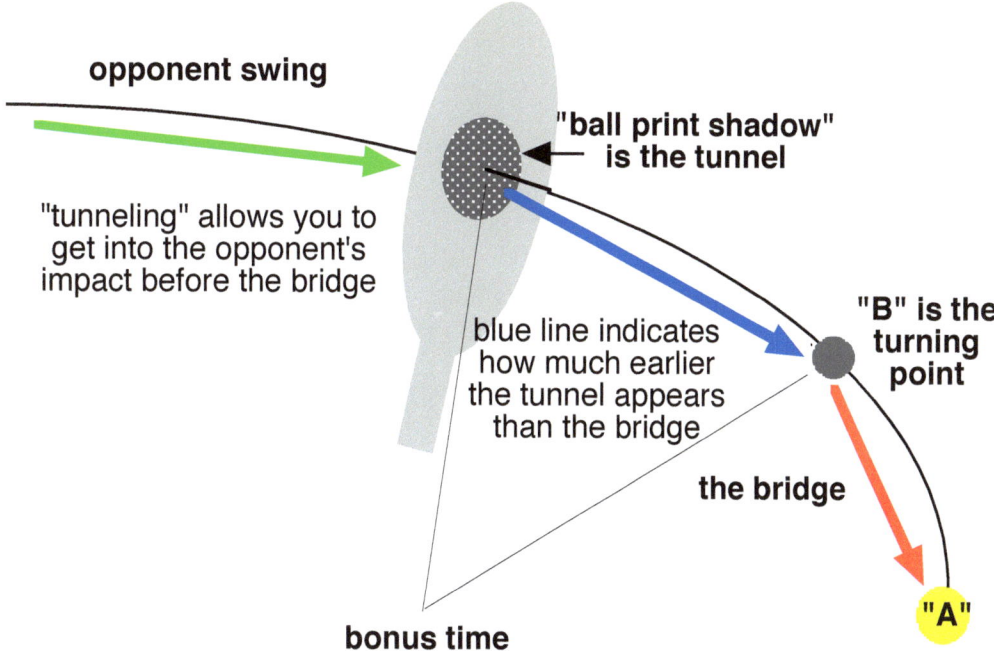

The idea of responding to the earliest information possible has created the "tunnel" focus model. The opponent starts his back swing and your sight-line follows his racket with till it stops at the end of the back swing. The moment the swing reverses into the forward swing you place a "ball print shadow" on the strings of the racket. This shadow is a mental construction that you create on the strings and is a future representation of the actual ball imprint at the impact. The ball print shadow's shape varies depending on the racket's approach angle to the ball. The shadow is the opening of your tunnel and allows you to generate a vector "c" by running a scalar bar through it. You can scalar the tunnel from the front (easiest access) or the back, by moving around to the other side of the impending impact. Either way you get your vector "c" before the bridge appears.

The earlier you perceive the opponent's intention the better.

←──────── tennis king "physics" ────────→

The "tunnel concept" permits you to obtain very accurate information pre-bridge.

TENNIS KING EQUATION² "BEYOND THE VORTEX"
OPTIMAL PLAY THROUGH "ENERGY FIELD" RECOGNITION

The tunnel appears before the bridge. It may not seem like it would make a difference, because the time frame is measured in milliseconds. But it makes a huge difference in the generation of your next response. In time and precision.

The "ball print shadow" is our mind casting the ball's shadow on to the opponent's strings, just the same way a spot light set up behind the ball would do. The racket's angle at the moment the shadow appears creates difference shadow shapes and these shapes determine the type of shot that you come up with. A round shadow means the opponent's next shot is flat and oval shadow that is leaning backward is a slice or leaning forward is topspin. This level of detail produces the quickest and easiest shots for you to hit.

If you have a choice between the bridge or tunnel - take the tunnel - it's faster.

TENNIS KING EQUATION ^{2} "BEYOND THE VORTEX"
OPTIMAL PLAY THROUGH "ENERGY FIELD" RECOGNITION

"TENNIS KING EQUATION 2" WRITTEN BY HEAD PRO MARK JOHNS ESPECIALLY FOR YOU.

TUNNEL VISION & TIME TUNNELING

REALISE YOUR SHOT POTENTIAL BY USING A TRIANGLE AT THE TUNNEL ENTRANCE

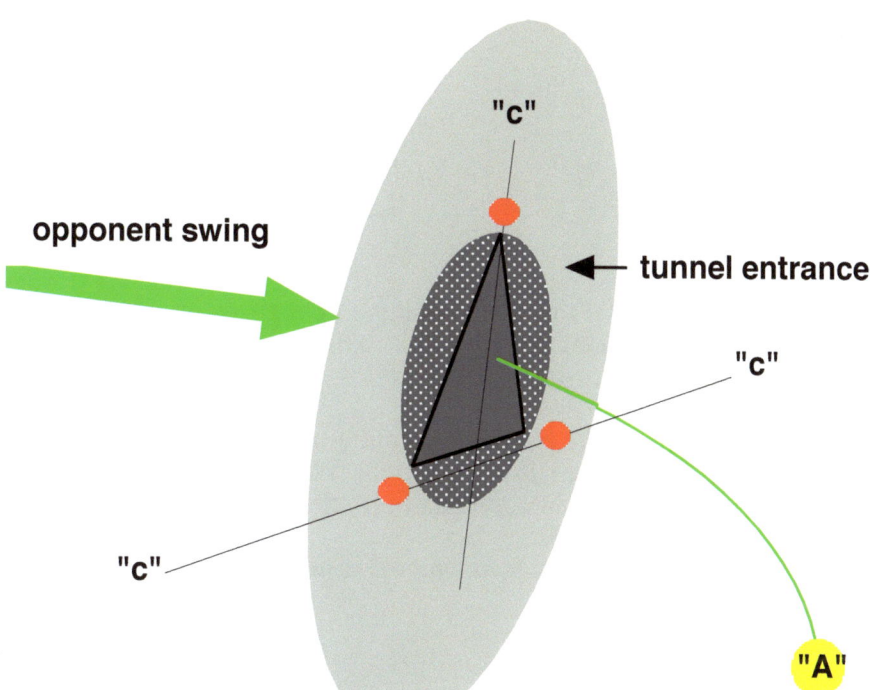

The tunnel entrance is determined by the ball print shadow on the racket face at the moment the swing changes from back swing to forward swing. The shadow is a configuration created by the angle of the racket's approach to the ball.

The entrance or the opening of the tunnel is best measured by placing a triangle on this shadow with the top of the triangle at 12:00. The 3 vertices of the triangle serve as guides for the shot selection. The top point equals a shot directly back to the opponent and the two bottom corners are equivalent to the total range of vector "c" addresses across the entire court.

Follow the opponent's back swing and then determine the tunnel entrance on the racket.

⬅ ***tennis king "physics"*** ➡

Triangulate the tunnel to allow you 3 possible vector addresses.

TENNIS KING EQUATION ^{2} "BEYOND THE VORTEX"
OPTIMAL PLAY THROUGH "ENERGY FIELD" RECOGNITION

The idea that you can determine where the shot is going and begin your shot before the opponent even hits the ball is a way to undermined your opponent's sense of control. The collapsing time frame can rush the opponent into unforced errors.

You can also take physical control of the point by selecting one of the triangle's vertices to create your vector "c" address to it's maximum potential. When you max out every shot physically you can run the opponent into the ground.

The power of the triangle is increased when it resides in the tunnel.

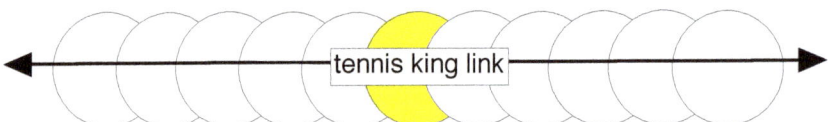

TENNIS KING EQUATION ^{2} "BEYOND THE VORTEX"
OPTIMAL PLAY THROUGH "ENERGY FIELD" RECOGNITION

"TENNIS KING EQUATION 2" WRITTEN BY HEAD PRO MARK JOHNS ESPECIALLY FOR YOU.

"LOAD-LOCK-HOLD" IS ALL YOU HAVE TO DO

THE PROCESS OF TUNNELING CAN BE REDUCED TO TO 3 FUNCTIONS

Once you are in the tunnel - look for the triangle. One of the 3 vertices of the triangle is going to become the vector address for your next shot. Each vertex offers you a shot with a specific purpose.

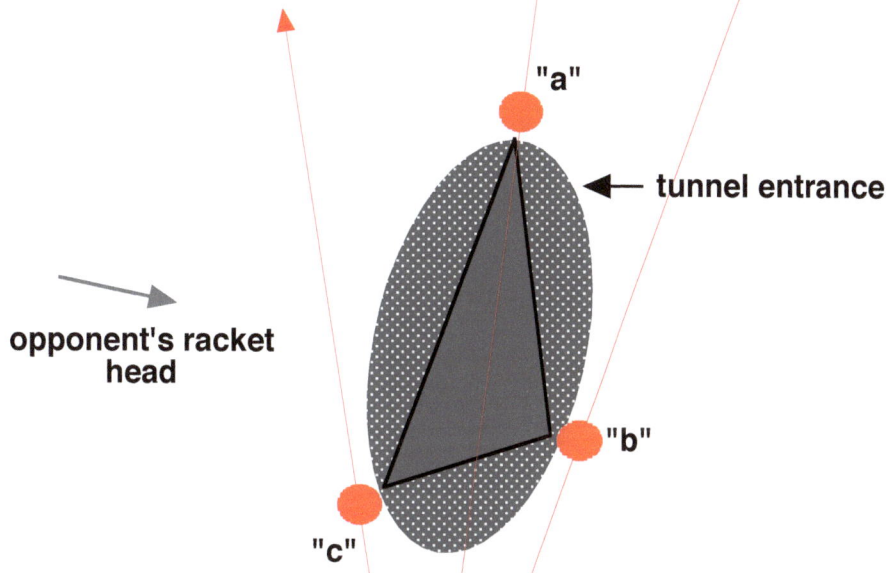

Vertex "a" is a recycling address for hitting down the middle of the court or back to the opponent. Vertex "b" is going to run your opponent into a corner and give you time to attack on the next shot. Vertex "c" is for passing shots and out right winners. This address compresses time and rushes your opponent. Use this address for ending the point.

Your shot production is simply a matter of loading a vertex into your conscious mind. Then locking it in as the vector address and holding it till your shot is complete.

The tunnel triangle defines your shot selection with it's vertices.

← ***tennis king "physics"*** →

The vector address is produced by loading - locking and holding the vertex.

TENNIS KING EQUATION² "BEYOND THE VORTEX"

OPTIMAL PLAY THROUGH "ENERGY FIELD" RECOGNITION

In the "load-lock-hold" concept, which component do you think is the most difficult to maintain? While everyone is capable of mastering this process, the part about the "hold" is where a problem is most likely to occur.

The idea of "loading" our conscious mind with one of the vertices is very exciting, it is the easiest to accomplish. The "locking" phase is slightly more involved because requires that you convert one of the vertices "a-b-c" into a vector address. This is simple to do so the player is still ok. The "hold" is where the conscious mind and it's will power are tested the most. To hold the vector address means allowing no other distraction to cross your mind. The player also has to physically pursue this vector address during the holding phase without "crossing over".

Creating a vector address is easy - holding on to it is another story!

TENNIS KING EQUATION^2 "BEYOND THE VORTEX"
OPTIMAL PLAY THROUGH "ENERGY FIELD" RECOGNITION

"TENNIS KING EQUATION 2" WRITTEN BY HEAD PRO MARK JOHNS ESPECIALLY FOR YOU.

STREAMLINING THE TUNNEL'S TRIANGLE

THE MERCEDES BENZ'S SYMBOL BECOMES A QUICK TARGETING ICON

The pre-bridge tunnel is a fast route to the vector address. The "tri-star" is an even quicker consolidation of the tunnel's triangle. The "tri-star" symbol is the Mercedes Benz's logo placed on the tunnel triangle's vertices. Each bisector line ends in a possible vector address.

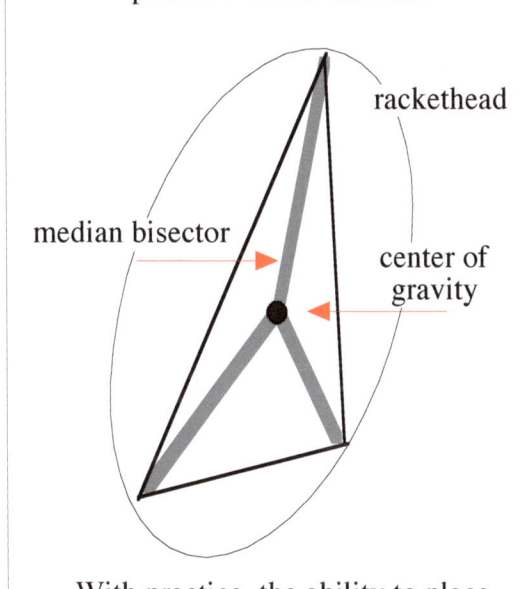

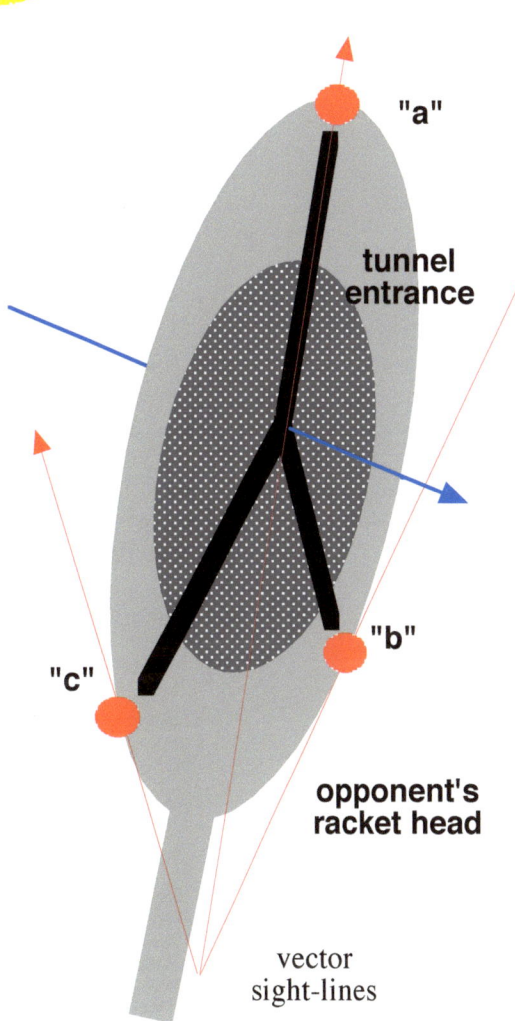

With practice, the ability to place the tri-star on the opponent's rackethead as it reaches the end of the back swing provides a quick target system for vectoring.

Quick and accurate is the criteria for an excellent focus model.

◄──── tennis king "physics" ────►

The tripod is a super fast model with the addition benefit of footwork enhancement.

TENNIS KING EQUATION² "BEYOND THE VORTEX"
OPTIMAL PLAY THROUGH "ENERGY FIELD" RECOGNITION

The "tri-star" icon is located just before the "vortex bridge" in the 3rd dimension of time. On the time line this is as far into the physical landscape you can go to generate a predictable focus reference for your vector address.

The recognition of the ball print shadow now converted into the tri-star also includes a footwork characteristic. The player who projects the tri-star on to the opponent's racket face can be more effective if he follows the trajectory of his previous shot till it bounces on the opponent's side. This positions the player at a point in the court where he can observe the tunnel and tri-star easily.

This point is located on the meridian line in the cone of opportunity.

"TENNIS KING EQUATION 2" WRITTEN BY HEAD PRO MARK JOHNS ESPECIALLY FOR YOU.

5

"THE EYE OF TIME"

TENNIS KING EQUATION ^{2} "BEYOND THE VORTEX"
OPTIMAL PLAY THROUGH "ENERGY FIELD" RECOGNITION

The Tennis King terminology:

the eye of time & moment of ignition = the point when time produces a physical energy.

vortical flow = the conversion of time's energy into physical energy.

vortical spectrum = a spectral measurement for the flow of time & physical energy in the opponent's body

nucleus of vortical flow = the point where the energy of time converts to physical energy on the vortical spectrum.

nuclear ring = the circumference of the vortical nucleus, used to generate vector addresses.

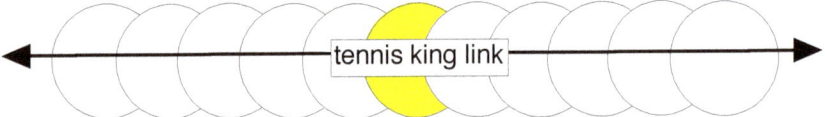

TENNIS KING EQUATION^2 "BEYOND THE VORTEX"
OPTIMAL PLAY THROUGH "ENERGY FIELD" RECOGNITION

"TENNIS KING EQUATION 2" WRITTEN BY HEAD PRO MARK JOHNS ESPECIALLY FOR YOU.

THE "VORTICAL FLOW" AND "THE EYE OF TIME"

THE FABRIC OF TIME RUNS INTO THE EYE OF TIME AND VORTICAL FLOW COMES OUT.

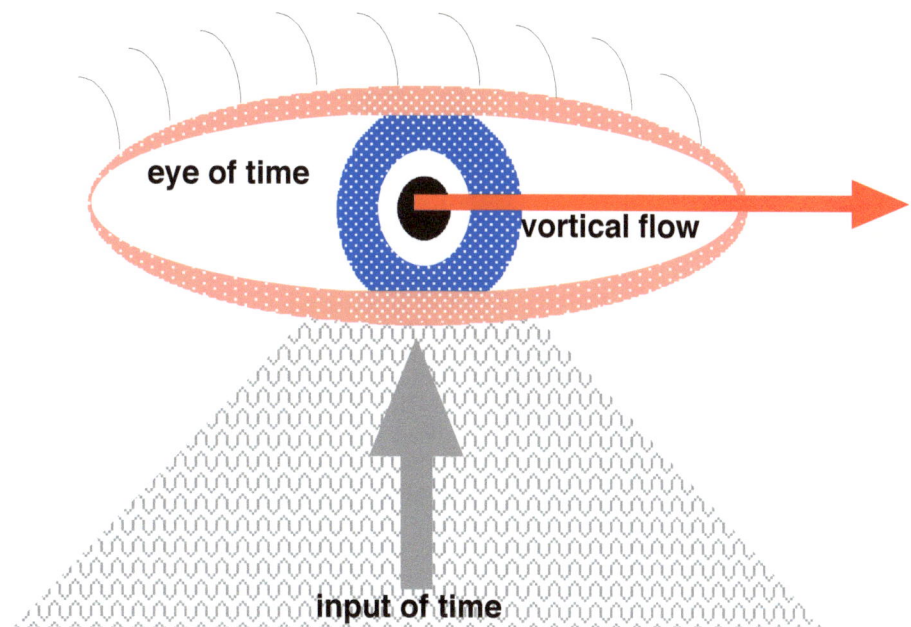

Time is the foundation of all action. Time converts into vortical flow as it funnels through the eye of time. Vortical flow is the energy of actions that in turn defines physical space. When a player allows his "mind's eye" to see vortical flow, the construction of physical space is understood. This understanding is all that is required to respond in time to the physical action of the opponent hitting the ball.

The "eye of time" and the "vortical flow" can not be seen visually .
← **tennis king "physics"** →
You can see them only with in your mind - you can not see them with your brain.

TENNIS KING EQUATION² "BEYOND THE VORTEX"
OPTIMAL PLAY THROUGH "ENERGY FIELD" RECOGNITION

The beauty of this game is when everything fits together perfectly. This is the object of our desire. To gain an understanding of the situation and to work it out in our favor.

The player can only achieve this end through an awareness of the relationship between time and energy. The formula of e=mc2 (energy = mass x speed of light squared) is the backbone of Einstein's special relativity theory. The Tennis King applies it like this.

The Tennis King Equation2 is based on time = the speed of light (c) divided by (m) "moment of ignition" represented by the "eye of time" equals (vf) or vortical flow. The "vortical flow" in this case represents the opponent's physical intention.

So "The Tennis King Equation2" is expressed as the following: vf = c/m

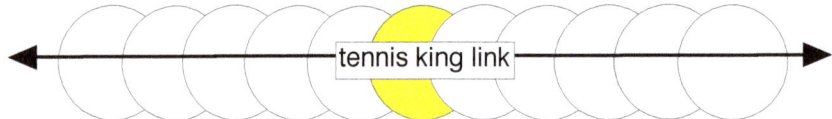

TENNIS KING EQUATION ^{2} "BEYOND THE VORTEX"
OPTIMAL PLAY THROUGH "ENERGY FIELD" RECOGNITION

"TENNIS KING EQUATION 2" WRITTEN BY HEAD PRO MARK JOHNS ESPECIALLY FOR YOU.

GET INTO "THE EYE OF TIME"

THE OPPONENT'S SHOT IS THE RESULT OF A PRE SWING "POINT OF IGNITION."

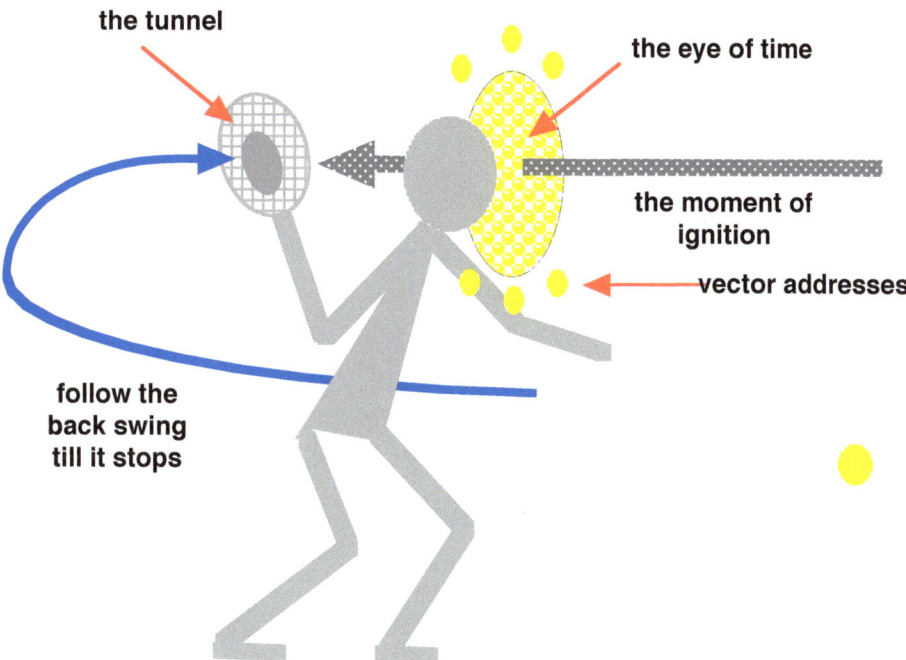

The "eye of time" is located in the mind of the opponent. The "eye of time" is the source of the tunnel and marks the moment that the forward swing is energized.

Find the eye by following the back swing till it stops and wait to feel the surge of power begin in the opponent's body. You can sense this energy before you see a physical movement. This release of energy is the "moment of ignition" of vortical flow. Once this point is realized you can apply your address system. Shown above is the six vector address system.

It is in the stillness of the "eye of time" that the shot is born.

⬅ *tennis king "physics"* ➡

Like being in the eye of the storm - a calmness envelops you as the vectors appear.

TENNIS KING EQUATION ^{2} "BEYOND THE VORTEX"
OPTIMAL PLAY THROUGH "ENERGY FIELD" RECOGNITION

There is the feeling of "strange calmness" when you are in the "eye of time". This calmness is a critical characteristic that must be experienced to qualify a player as being in the eye of time. Once you are there, time will stand still while you apply your address system. Any focus model will work in the eye of time.

The address systems that you may apply in the eye of time are placed on to the surge of energy within the opponent (vortical flow) as they begin the physical effort to hit the ball. This moment of truth is only available in the eye of time and it is not seen or felt with a visual eye, but rather the "mind's eye".

To access to the "eye of time" you need to apply the "eye of mind".

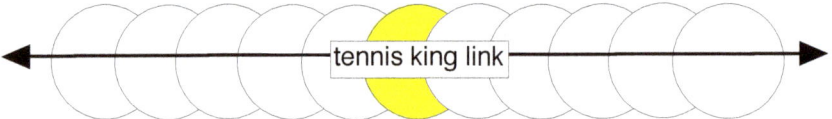

TENNIS KING EQUATION^2 "BEYOND THE VORTEX"
OPTIMAL PLAY THROUGH "ENERGY FIELD" RECOGNITION

"TENNIS KING EQUATION 2" WRITTEN BY HEAD PRO MARK JOHNS ESPECIALLY FOR YOU.

ZOOM INTO THE "VORTICAL FLOW" SPECTRUM

CHARTING VORTICAL FLOW IS LIKE RIDING IN A HIGH SPEED ELEVATOR - YOU ARE THERE IN NO TIME.

The idea of "vortical flow" is very intuitive. It is recognized with the "mind's eye" as the energy running from the earth through the opponent's body.

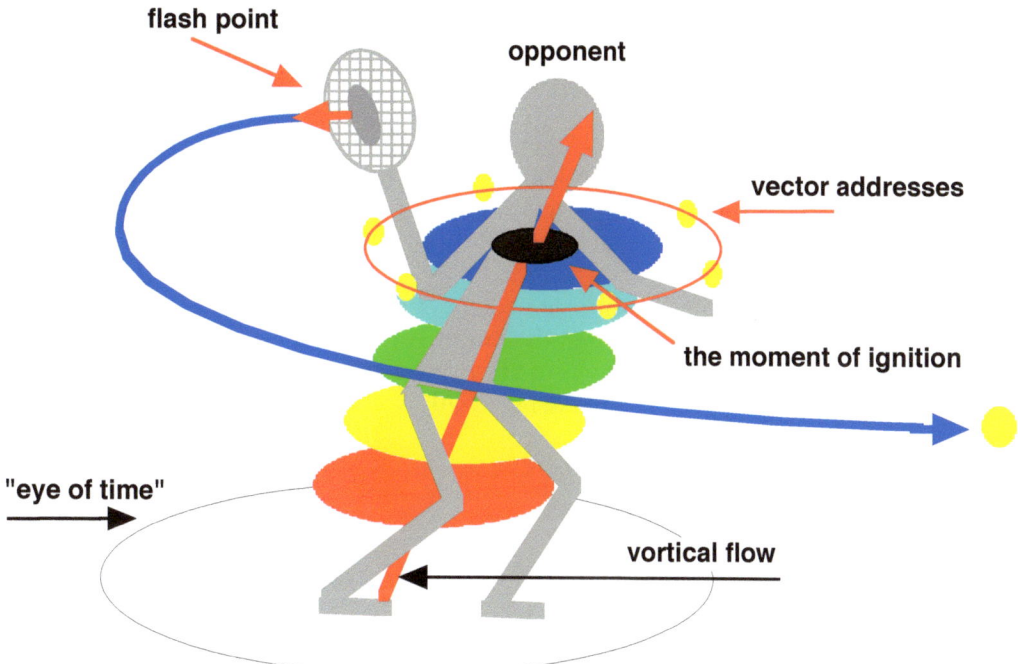

Think of the vortical flow as an energy elevator moving upward and divided into a "five level spectrum of intensities. Each level has a different energy level and shot making capabilities. Shown above is a level 5 "moment of ignition".

The bottom level has the longest wavelength and produces big shots that will force you to match the energy, limiting shot selection. The middle range levels are less powerful and allow you to manipulate the energy more. The top levels are very short wave lengths like drop shots, volleys and weak shots. You can really do a lot with these if you can detect them early enough.

The energy spectrum of vortical flow is perfect for instantaneous responses.

← tennis king "physics" →

Moment of ignition is the center of the vector radius and the level determines your shot.

TENNIS KING EQUATION^2 "BEYOND THE VORTEX"
OPTIMAL PLAY THROUGH "ENERGY FIELD" RECOGNITION

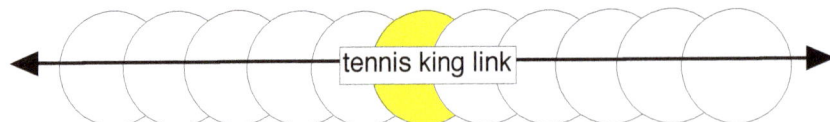

The spectrum of energy runs from bottom to top, with the bottom levels more powerful and the top more sensitive or softer. This is going to be determined by where the "moment of ignition" occurs. A surge of energy runs upward within the opponent as "vortical flow" till it reach a point on the spectrum and stops.

The "moment of ignition" converts into physical action. This physical action is noted as the "flash point". In the interim between the "moment of ignition" and the "flash point" you generate the vector address and begin your physical response before the opponent strikes the ball.

Start at the bottom and follow the vortical flow till the "moment of ignition" - bingo!

TENNIS KING EQUATION ^{2} "BEYOND THE VORTEX"
OPTIMAL PLAY THROUGH "ENERGY FIELD" RECOGNITION

"TENNIS KING EQUATION 2" WRITTEN BY HEAD PRO MARK JOHNS ESPECIALLY FOR YOU.

DEVELOP THE URGE TO CHANNEL THE SURGE

THE MOMENT OF IGNITION IS THE VECTOR'S EPICENTER IN THE SURGE OF VORTICAL FLOW

The "moment of ignition" is the recognition of energy surging in the opponent when he moves to hit the ball. This surge's exact "moment and level" in the vortical flow is measured by it's occurrence in relation to the on coming ball.

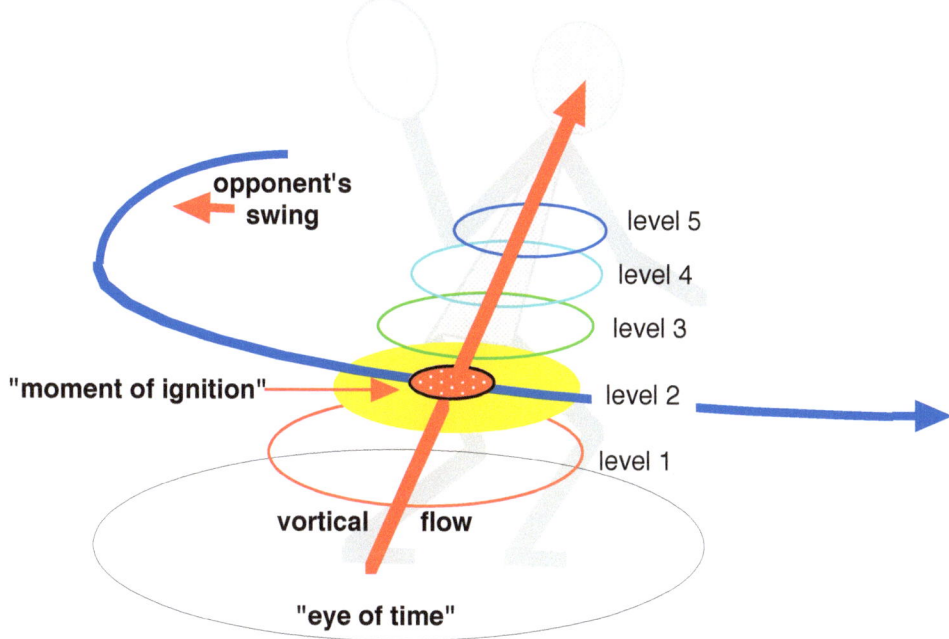

As the ball closes in on the opponent a surge of energy is observed by watching the opponent move to the ball. The "moment of ignition" is determined by when the energy for the swing begins within the opponent's body. If the moment of ignition occurs very early, this would equal a level 1 in the vortical flow and the opponent would actually hit the ball very early and with much power. The spectrum of vortical continues till a moment of ignition occurs and as it flows higher into the body the energy level lessens. At level 5 you would be experiencing maybe a drop shot or a short shot.

The level of ignition determines the possibilities that exist for shot selection.

tennis king "physics"

Lower levels have less options and higher levels have more options for shotmaking.

TENNIS KING EQUATION^2 "BEYOND THE VORTEX"
OPTIMAL PLAY THROUGH "ENERGY FIELD" RECOGNITION

The observation of vortical flow is acquired by learning to watch the opponent preparing to hit the ball in a certain way. The visual focus is adjusted to capture the overall event, starting at the ball's bounce and continuing through the swing and impact of the ball.

With help from your mind's imagination the "surge" or rise of vortical flow is tracked from ground level up into the opponent's body till it reaches the "point of ignition". The higher the energy rises on the vortical spectrum the weaker the opponent's response.

The level of vortical flow determines the physical potential.

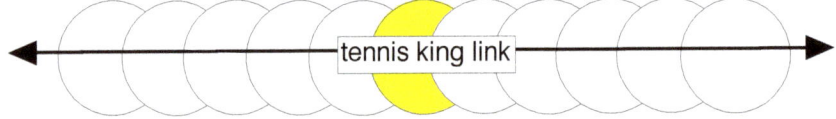

TENNIS KING EQUATION^2 "BEYOND THE VORTEX"
OPTIMAL PLAY THROUGH "ENERGY FIELD" RECOGNITION

"TENNIS KING EQUATION 2" WRITTEN BY HEAD PRO MARK JOHNS ESPECIALLY FOR YOU.

YOU HAVE TO GO "NUCLEAR" TO BE ATOMIC

THE MOMENT OF IGNITION IS THE NUCLEUS OF THE THE OPPONENT'S SHOT

The view below is the opponent and vortical flow as it reaches ignition. The moment of ignition becomes the "nucleus" of the shot and the surrounding "electrons" are potential vector addresses. Remember this is a mental construction that occupies your conscious mind created by your imagination and seen in the "mind's eye".

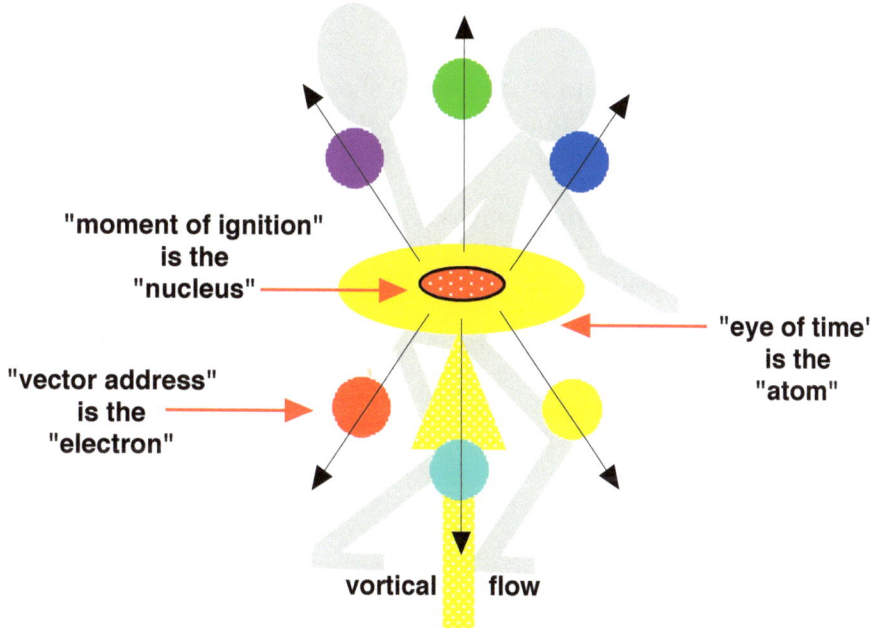

The "nucleus" of the shot is the start of the forward swing to hit the ball. This nucleus is extremely important to the construction of your next shot. This nucleus is seen in your consciousness, but it is also projected on to the body of your opponent and occurs on one of the five levels of the vortical spectrum. To align your focus and your body to this nucleus, point your sight-line at the nucleus. This action will pull you and your swing into a synchronization with the time frame.

The conversion of the "moment of ignition" into a nucleus allows for a vector selection.

⬅ *tennis king "physics"* ➡

The "electron" vector is singled out by the knuckle focusing on it - creating an address.

TENNIS KING EQUATION² "BEYOND THE VORTEX"
OPTIMAL PLAY THROUGH "ENERGY FIELD" RECOGNITION

The vortical flow transformation into an atom with six electrons seems pretty far out. That this is happening during actual point play with a second between impacts would seem to be impossible. It's not.

The mind that is programmed in a certain way is capable of this vectorization process. It can do it in 10 milliseconds leaving plenty of time to physically to hit the ball. This programming is just a matter of seeing the focus model and nothing else.

The degree of detail in the "atomic" vector model determines the quality of play.

TENNIS KING EQUATION^2 "BEYOND THE VORTEX"
OPTIMAL PLAY THROUGH "ENERGY FIELD" RECOGNITION

"TENNIS KING EQUATION 2" WRITTEN BY HEAD PRO MARK JOHNS ESPECIALLY FOR YOU.

TO CREATE AN IMPACT - STEP INTO THE RING

RESPOND TO THE VORTICAL FLOW BY MOVING FORWARD INTO THE OPPONENT'S SHOT NUCLEUS

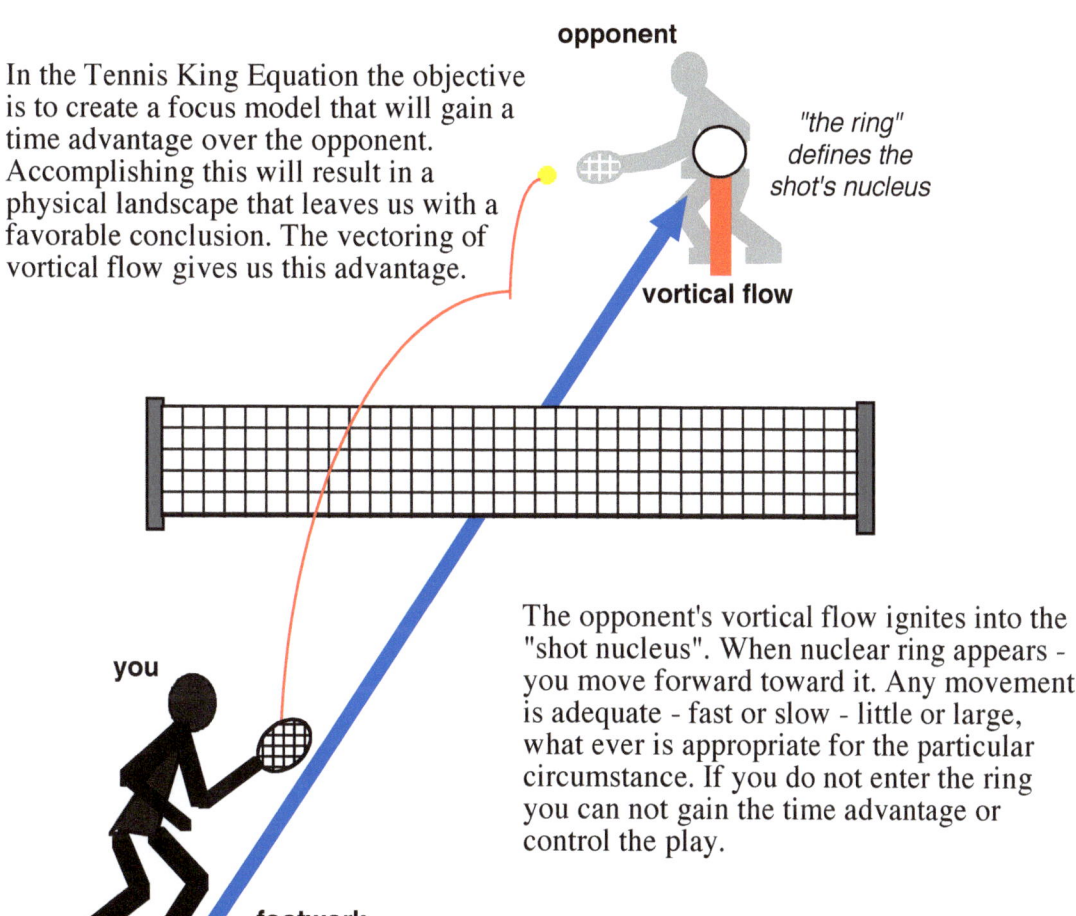

In the Tennis King Equation the objective is to create a focus model that will gain a time advantage over the opponent. Accomplishing this will result in a physical landscape that leaves us with a favorable conclusion. The vectoring of vortical flow gives us this advantage.

The opponent's vortical flow ignites into the "shot nucleus". When nuclear ring appears - you move forward toward it. Any movement is adequate - fast or slow - little or large, what ever is appropriate for the particular circumstance. If you do not enter the ring you can not gain the time advantage or control the play.

By moving forward the player accesses a position to optimize the vector address.

← tennis king "physics" →

The position obtained also allows for a continuous closing of the court.

TENNIS KING EQUATION² "BEYOND THE VORTEX"
OPTIMAL PLAY THROUGH "ENERGY FIELD" RECOGNITION

The time over space advantage requires that you see into the future and act on this information rather then react to the physical reality. Every focus model that we have engineered takes us further out into the future.

The examination of vortical flow is realized in a conscious minded visualization. It is based on numerous variables absorbed during the play. The unconscious mind accumulates and processes this information without the hesitation that can occur in the conscious mind.

It is not a risk to trust the your instincts - it is a risk not trusting them.

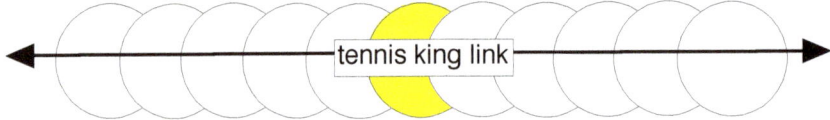

TENNIS KING EQUATION ^{2} "BEYOND THE VORTEX"
OPTIMAL PLAY THROUGH "ENERGY FIELD" RECOGNITION

"TENNIS KING EQUATION 2" WRITTEN BY HEAD PRO MARK JOHNS ESPECIALLY FOR YOU.

THE SHOT'S NUCLEUS = THE NUCLEAR CLOCK

YOUR GAME WILL RUN LIKE CLOCK WORK ON A SUBATOMIC LEVEL BY WATCHING VORTICAL FLOW

The vortical flow ignites into the shot's nucleus on a level of the vortical spectrum, providing the opportunity to see the nucleus' ring as a "vector clock". This nuclear vector clock will provide an address for your next shot that will be ahead of the opponent's impact. This extremely early addressing allows you to physically start hitting your shot before the opponent has hit his. See the clock early and you are good to go.

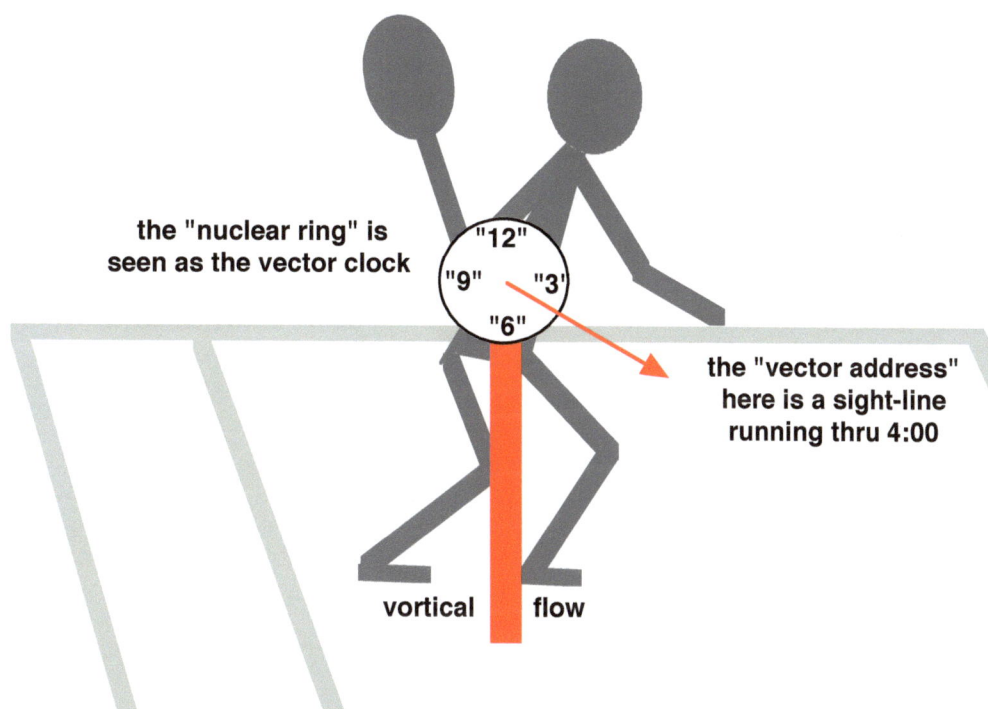

The return of the vector clock provides a level of extreme precision to hit the shot.

← ***tennis king "physics"*** →

Now the level of precision is combined with a very early dimension of time.

TENNIS KING EQUATION ^{2} "BEYOND THE VORTEX"
OPTIMAL PLAY THROUGH "ENERGY FIELD" RECOGNITION

Once again the clock is back in the focus model. An address system using a vector clock provides a level of precision that is extreme and dependable. In this focus model the vector clock is located in the opponent's vortical flow.

This nuclear clock location is very forward in time. This places you way ahead of your opponent. Holding the "vector clock" address throughout the process of hitting your shot will guarantee a perfect placement.

The nuclear clock is the way to exploit your opponent's vortical flow.

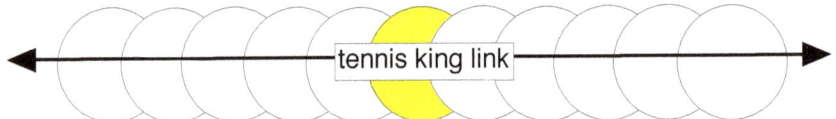

TENNIS KING EQUATION ^{2} "BEYOND THE VORTEX"
OPTIMAL PLAY THROUGH "ENERGY FIELD" RECOGNITION

"TENNIS KING EQUATION 2" WRITTEN BY HEAD PRO MARK JOHNS ESPECIALLY FOR YOU.

6

"VORTIVISION" AND "VECTOR FIELDS"

TENNIS KING EQUATION ^{2} "BEYOND THE VORTEX"
OPTIMAL PLAY THROUGH "ENERGY FIELD" RECOGNITION

The Tennis King terminology:

vortivision = a focus which is totally devoted to tracking vortical flow.

vector fields = fields of vector addresses which are generated by vortivision.

vortical spectrum = a spectral measurement for the flow of time & physical energy in the opponent's body

nucleus of vortical flow = the point where the energy of time converts to physical energy on the vortical spectrum.

nuclear ring = the circumference of the vortical nucleus, used to generate vector addresses.

alpha-beta moment = the exact time information moves from the mind into the brain.

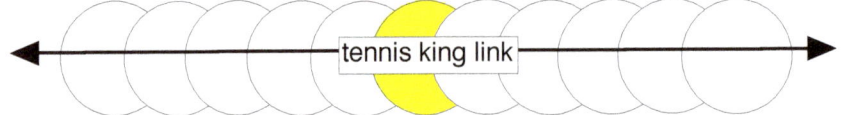

TENNIS KING EQUATION² "BEYOND THE VORTEX"
OPTIMAL PLAY THROUGH "ENERGY FIELD" RECOGNITION

"TENNIS KING EQUATION 2" WRITTEN BY HEAD PRO MARK JOHNS ESPECIALLY FOR YOU.

VORTIVISION TRACKS VORTICAL FLOW

VORTIVSION IS THE MOST PREDATORY OF FOCUS MODELS - IT TRACKS THE OPPONENT NOT THE BALL.

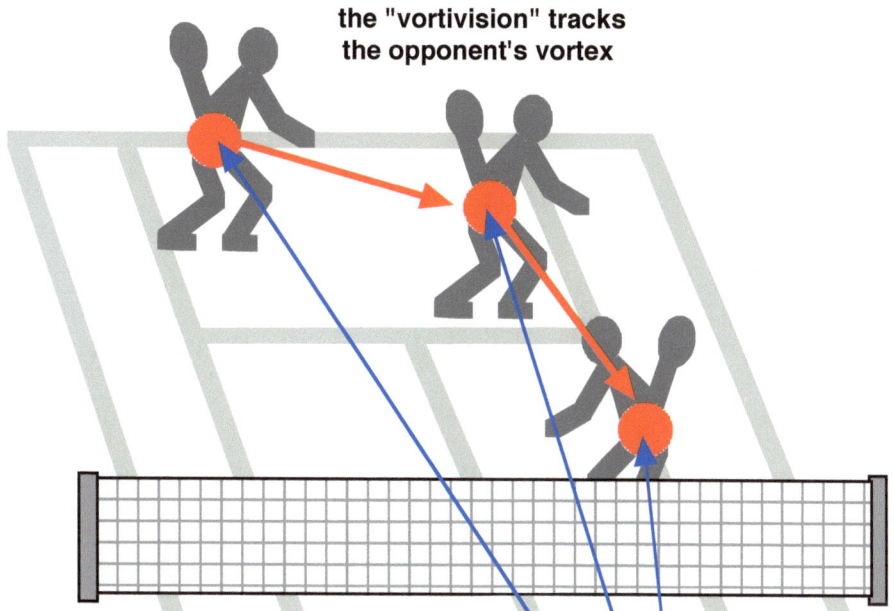

the "vortivision" tracks the opponent's vortex

In this focus model you track the opponent down by attaching a vortivision sight-line on the vortex nucleus. As the opponent moves around the court the you follow the vortex till it reaches the "moment of ignition". Once the nuclear ring is clear you produce the vector address by moving vortivision through the open nucleus ring to the vector destination. The process is completed by holding open the nuclear ring till the ball comes off your racket. Then you recycle your vortivision on the opponent and continue to play the point.

The vortivision sight-line is a product of the mind's eye focus on the nuclear ring.

← *tennis king "physics"* →

In order to maintain vortivision you need to let go of conscious visual references.

TENNIS KING EQUATION ² "BEYOND THE VORTEX"
OPTIMAL PLAY THROUGH "ENERGY FIELD" RECOGNITION

The ability to let go of conscious minded visual references to follow vortical flow is vortivision. It is a state of mind where you are responding to an overall energy field and not singling out any one specific moment or physical action other then the vortex.

The opponent's vortical nucleus is available to you only when your own vortex energy is calm and quiet. Vortivision is founded on your own energy as much as your opponent's. When you try to force the focus the opponent's vortical flow will disappear.

To stay in the vortical flow you need to liquify your own vortical energy.

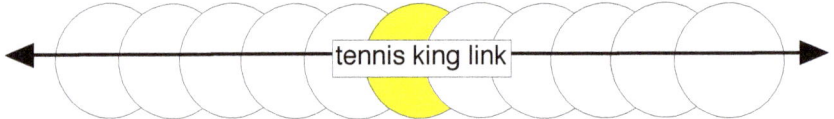

TENNIS KING EQUATION ^{2} "BEYOND THE VORTEX"
OPTIMAL PLAY THROUGH "ENERGY FIELD" RECOGNITION

"TENNIS KING EQUATION 2" WRITTEN BY HEAD PRO MARK JOHNS ESPECIALLY FOR YOU.

VORTIVISION - NUCLEAR RING - THE FUTURE

THE VORTIVISION SIGHT-LINE PRODUCES THE SCALAR BAR FOR THE VECTOR "C".

This diagram is defining a nuclear ring at the moment of ignition. Any one of the blue vortivision sight-lines could be your view into the the nuclear ring. The sight-line reaches the connecting point on the ring generates a scalar bar which in turn brings you to vector "c". The vector "c" is the future destination of your response to this shot being hit here.

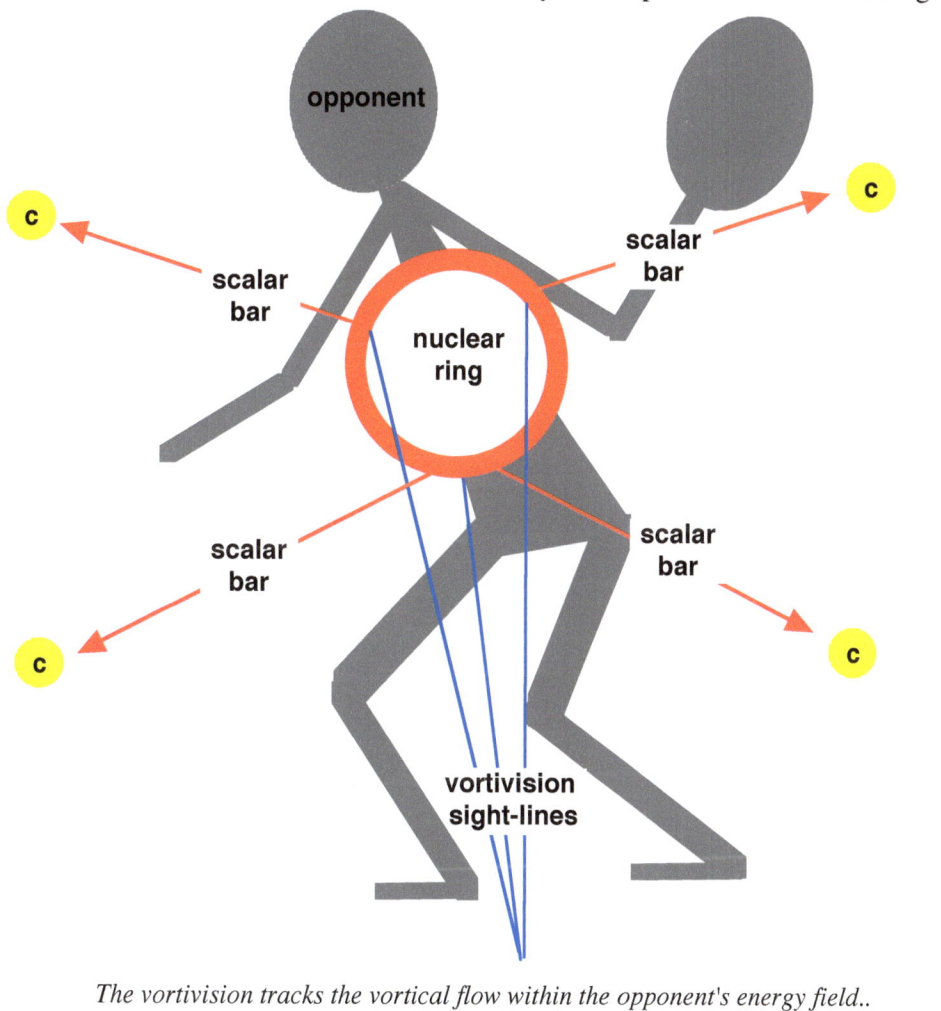

The vortivision tracks the vortical flow within the opponent's energy field..

tennis king *"physics"*

It also produces the scalar bar that leads to the vector "c" of your shot.

TENNIS KING EQUATION ² "BEYOND THE VORTEX"
OPTIMAL PLAY THROUGH "ENERGY FIELD" RECOGNITION

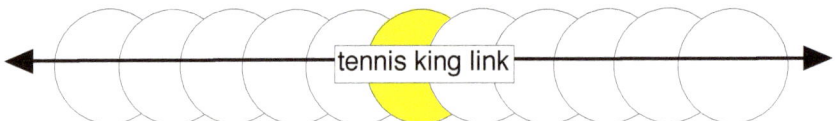

The **vortical flow** produces in the - **moment of ignition** - the - **nuclear ring**. The ring is the primary target for our focus sight-line. This sight-line is the result of our **vortivision**.

The object of vortivision is to bring us to our **vector "c"** before the opponent hits the ball. The sight-line hits the nuclear ring and converts into a **scalar bar**. It is this scalar bar that brings use to vector "c". The vector "c" then attracts our shot to it's location.

This entire process occurs in the "alpha-beta" moment in our mind.

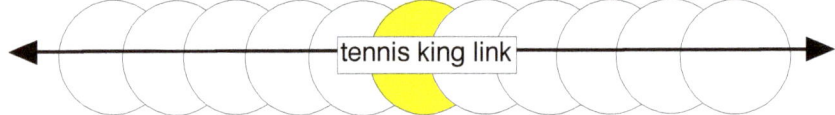

TENNIS KING EQUATION^2 "BEYOND THE VORTEX"
OPTIMAL PLAY THROUGH "ENERGY FIELD" RECOGNITION

"TENNIS KING EQUATION 2" WRITTEN BY HEAD PRO MARK JOHNS ESPECIALLY FOR YOU.

THE VECTOR FIELD TRIGGERS THE ALPHA-BETA

THE ALPHA-BETA MOMENT IS THE CONVERTING FACTOR IN THE TIME-SPACE CONTINUUM.

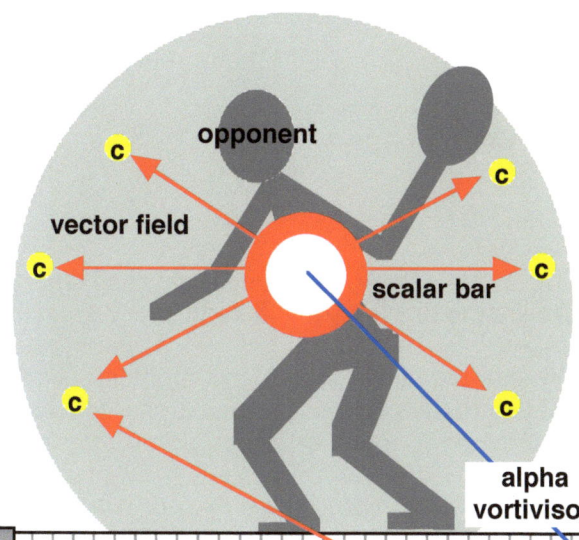

The vector field (the gray circle) is defined by possible vector addresses located at the end of the scalar bars. The vortivision is an alpha focus wave. This sight-line comes from our mind's eye and is attached to the nuclear ring. Our ability to create the alpha state of mind is the core of the game we bring to the match.

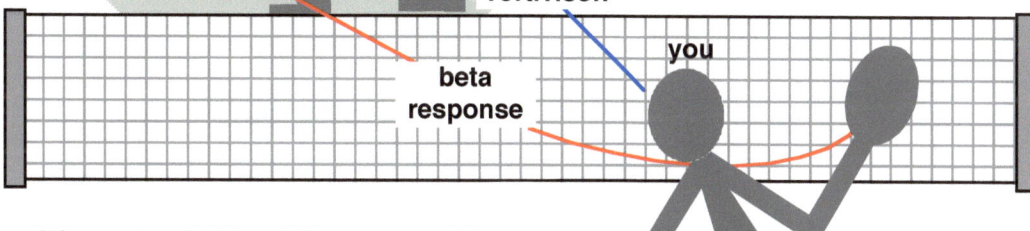

The vector field and the vector address are the alpha state's product. The beta response is the physical action of hitting the shot. This alpha-beta transaction is the total coordination of the mind and brain working together. Once the mind recognizes the vector address the brain's motor cortex fires off the physical reply.

Alpha state is a low frequency of brain wave and beta state is a higher frequency wave.

← *tennis king "physics"* →

Once again the "mind over matter" realization is proven to conquer the physical game.

TENNIS KING EQUATION ^{2} "BEYOND THE VORTEX"
OPTIMAL PLAY THROUGH "ENERGY FIELD" RECOGNITION

The tennis player's greatest asset is not the athletic body, foot speed, physical strength. It is the mind. The player's **brain and mind** are the driving force behind every great player.

The **alpha-beta moment** occurs in every shot the player hits. If this moment is composed correctly, everything falls into place. When **distraction** reigns this alpha-beta response misfires and errors result. Coordinate the mind to the brain and you have it right.

The alpha-beta response is the moment of truth for every shot you hit.

TENNIS KING EQUATION^2 "BEYOND THE VORTEX"
OPTIMAL PLAY THROUGH "ENERGY FIELD" RECOGNITION

"TENNIS KING EQUATION 2" WRITTEN BY HEAD PRO MARK JOHNS ESPECIALLY FOR YOU.

THE TENNIS KING EQUATION2 - CONCLUSIONS

THE PHYSICAL PLAYER NEEDS A FOCUS MODEL THAT BECOMES AN OPERATING SYSTEM FOR THE MIND.

The Tennis King Equation2 is complete. These concepts of scalar focus has been recorded by the reader and it is now the time to digest the information that we have taken in.

We have read about focus models and operating systems. They are composed of vortexes and vectors, scalar focus waves and dimensions of time. You now have a half a dozen focus models to choose from. The black hole's "valley of compression", the "bridge and tunnel", the "golden triangle" and there are more - just go back and refresh your memory.

Operating systems differ from player to player and so they should. The trick is to find one that fits the current state of your physical game. Each model resides in a different dimension of time and when your game is ready - you just upgrade the focus model.

As the player moves farther into the future, the physical game fades into the subconscious. This is exacty what you want to happen. Each advanced dimension of time requires stronger focus skills and increased emotional commitment. The growth of a player's game is the reflection of the player's mind and who he is as a human being.

Tennis is one of the few activities where the player can continue to grow right up to the last day of play. Hopefully that last day is far out there in the future.

The Tennis King Equation does not end here. The next concept is coming up fast and it will be the subject of the next book:

The Tennis King Equation3 - Inner Peace = Inner Energy

Until the next equation is completed - just remember The Tennis King motto:

Play well to stay well!

Every day we play we learn something new - even if we don't realize it.

⬅———— *tennis king "physics"* ————➡

Where ever you are - in all dimensions of time - the answer to the question is with you.

TENNIS KING EQUATION² "BEYOND THE VORTEX"
OPTIMAL PLAY THROUGH "ENERGY FIELD" RECOGNITION

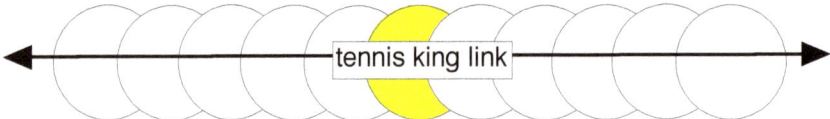

The The Tennis King Equation series is really written for just one person.
I know at the top of every page I state:

"TENNIS KING EQUATION" WRITTEN BY HEAD PRO MARK JOHNS ESPECIALLY FOR YOU.

This is not entirely true. I have written the books for me and my game.
So how can I still believe that the books are written especially for the reader also?

The reason is at the end of the day we are all the same.

What makes the world's top player and the kid hitting against the school wall the same?

We play because we want to.

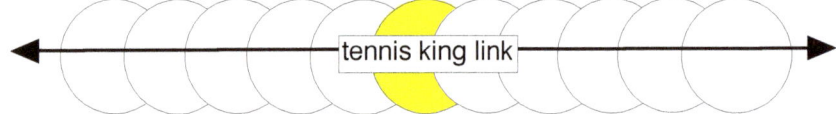

www.ingramcontent.com/pod-product-compliance
Lightning Source LLC
Chambersburg PA
CBHW041402020526
44115CB00036B/8